THE ANALOGY OF NAMES

and

THE CONCEPT OF BEING

THOMAS DE VIO, CARDINAL CAJETAN

THE ANALOGY OF NAMES
and
THE CONCEPT OF BEING

Literally Translated and Annotated by

EDWARD A. BUSHINSKI, C.S.Sp., M.A., S.T.L.

In Collaboration With

HENRY J. KOREN, C.S.Sp., S.T.D.

WIPF & STOCK · Eugene, Oregon

Wipf and Stock Publishers
199 W 8th Ave, Suite 3
Eugene, OR 97401

The Analogy of Names, and the Concept of Being
By Cajetan, Tommaso de Vio and Bushinski, Edward A.
ISBN 13: 978-1-60608-463-2
Publication date 1/19/2009
Previously published by Duquesne University, 1953

CONTENTS

APPENDIX

THE CONCEPT OF BEING

FOREWORD

Cajetan's well-known work *de Nominum Analogia* contains the first and still unsurpassed systematization of the Aristotelian-Thomistic theory of analogy. As such, it is the classical treatise of analogy and forms the basis of practically all modern discussions of the arduous problem of analogy.

The gratifying interest in Thomistic philosophy among scholars and students of philosophy whose knowledge of Latin is too restricted to study this work in the original language has prompted us to attempt its translation. Like the original, this translation lays no claim to literary merit; it is not destined for casual reading but only for prolonged and serious study. We have endeavored to express Cajetan's thought in a faithful and literal, yet intelligible, way. The profound metaphysical nature of the subject matter, together with Cajetan's complex and somewhat disconcerting style, did not make this an easy task. Complaints about the obscurity of his expression are voiced even by those whose knowledge of Latin leaves little to be desired.[1]

The actual work of the translation was done by Edward A. Bushinski, C.S.Sp., M.A., S.T.L. His work was thoroughly checked by the undersigned, who added most of the annotations and assumes full responsibility for the exactness of the whole work.

As regards the text, we have followed the edition prepared by P. N. Zammit, O.P., Rome, 1934, and revised by P. H. Hering, O.P., Rome, 1952. This critical edition is based upon the following four ancient editions:

Venetiis, *nonis Martii,* 1506
Parisiis, 1511
Lugdunensis, 1541
Venetiis, 1588.

Because of certain deficiencies of the first edition, the editors of the critical text generally have followed the Parisian edition of 1511.

The marginal numbers of the critical edition have been kept in this translation so as to facilitate references. However, we have not hesitated to deviate from the divisions of the critical edition when such a procedure appeared called for in order to make it easier to understand

[1]Cf. Melchior Cano, *Loci Theologici,* VI, 4.

the text. For the same reason subtitles have been added. Long titles of chapters have been abbreviated.

The annotations of this translation fall into the following categories:

1) Variant readings, indicated in the critical edition, which have some bearing upon the sense of the text.

2) Obscure passages, where the translators could not be entirely certain of the accuracy of their translation.

3) Proposed corrections of punctuation or of the text itself.

4) Pertinent quotations from authors cited or alluded to by Cajetan.

5) Excerpts from other works of Cajetan in which he speaks about the problems of analogy.

6) Quotations of St. Thomas, to show that Cajetan did not invent a new theory of analogy, but merely systematized the thought of St. Thomas.

7) A few explanatory notes, mostly taken from modern Thomistic philosophers.

8) References to modern controversies.

For some of these footnotes the annotations of the Zammit edition have been of great help. Most of them, however, are proper to this translation. Quotations from Aristotle have been indicated by their page, column and line in the Immanuel Bekker edition of Aristotle (Berlin, 1831). Their translation was taken from the Ross' edition of *The Works of Aristotle,* Oxford at the Clarendon Press, 1930, with kind permission of the publishers.

Words placed within square brackets are not found in the critical text, but added to the translation for the sake of clarity.

HENRY J. KOREN, C.S.Sp.

DUQUESNE UNIVERSITY

February 20, 1953, the 485th anniversary of the birth of Cajetan

INTRODUCTION*

The Life of Cajetan

The sixty-six years of Cajetan's life fall into a century of world-shattering events. Intrepid sailors, like Vasco da Gama and Columbus, opened up new worlds in the Far East and the West. Conquering Turkish armies swept over the South-Eastern part of Europe and threatened to engulf the whole West. His native Italy was torn by internal strife, while imperial troops of His Most Catholic Majesty, Emperor Charles the Fifth, sacked the Capital of Christendom. In France native Gallicanism endeavored to split the unity of the Church, in Germany a hitherto obscure monk nailed his theses to the church-doors of Wittenberg and started the Protestant Revolt, in England a lustful king proclamied himself Head of the Church, all over Europe the Church stood in urgent need of drastic reform.

Far from being a cloistered scholar, oblivious of the world at large and its problems, Cajetan played an active and important role in many. As one of the Church's greatest theologians, he wrote many works concerned with its immediate problems; as Master General of a religious order which fulfilled an important function in the life of the Church, he directed its activities against the errors of his time, promoted ecclesiastical discipline and unity, and sent missionaries to the New World; as a Counselor of four Popes, Julius II, Leo X, Adrian VI (in whose election he exercised perhaps decisive influence), and Clement VII, and as a Papal Legate, he dealt with such matters as the Pseudo-Council of Pisa and Luther himself. Notwithstanding all this activity he found time to write no less than 157 works of philosophy, theology and exegesis.

Thomas de Vio, better known as Cardinal Cajetan, was born at Gaeta, Italy, on February 20, 1468. At the age of 16 he entered the Order of Preachers, which sent him to study at Naples and Bologna. At the age of 23 he began his teaching career as a lector at Pavia. Two years later he became a Bachelor at the University of Padua and was appointed the task of interpreting the Books of Sentences.[1] In

*The historical data of this introduction have been taken from J. F. Groner, *Kardinal Cajetan,* Fribourg-Louvain, 1951, and P. Mandonnet, in *Dictionnaire de Théologie Catholique,* vol. II, Paris, 1930, col. 1313-1320.

[1]These commentaries have not yet been published.

1494 he received the Chair of Thomistic Metaphysics at the same university and promptly engaged in disputes against Antonius Trombetta, O. F. M., who held the Chair of Scotistic Metaphysics, and such Averroists as Pomponazzi and Vernias.[2] His intellectual capacities showed themselves in an event which happened in the year 1495. In that year the youthful Cajetan took part in a public disputation held at Ferrara. His opponent was the formidable Giovanni Francesco Pico della Mirandola, a humanist who had a violent dislike of anything Aristotelian. With a barrage of objections, each of which, so it seemed to his distinguished audience, was destined to strike terror into his frail and diminutive opponent, Pico tried to crush and confuse the supposedly unexperienced Bachelor. Cajetan's brilliance, however, was equal to the occasion. Undaunted by the display of Pico's artillery, he countered each objection with an appropriate distinction and brought Pico to shame. This performance caused such an enthusiasm among his hearers that they carried him in triumph to the seat of the Duke of Ferrara, who remarked that a man of such proven abilities need not wait any longer for the title of Master of Sacred Theology. Carried away by the general enthusiasm, the Dominican Master General Torriani took off his own Master's insignia and forthwith invested Cajetan, at the age of 26, as *Magister Sacrae Theologiae*.

In 1497 Cajetan was called by the Duke of Milan to teach theology at the University of Pavia. However, after two brief years he abandoned the university and spent the later part of 1499 and all of 1500 at a convent in Milan.

Upon the death of the Procurator General of the Order in 1500 Cajetan was named to occupy the vacant position. This new office forced him to move to Rome, and it was this turn of events which gave him occasion to perform brilliantly in public discourses and sermons before Popes Alexander VI and Julius II. At the death of Bandelli, the Master General of the Order, in 1509, the Pope appointed him Vicar General, and in 1510 the Chapter General of the Order, upon the strong recommendations of Cardinal Carafa, elected him, at the age of forty, Master General of the Order. In this new capacity he dedicated all his strength to restore discipline and zeal of learning among his confreres. In 1517 Pope Julius II made him a Cardinal, which did not prevent Cajetan from continuing to govern his Order. He wrote

---

[2]These disputes resulted in his commentaries on *de Ente et Essentia*.

magnificent circular letters, took part in important councils and performed other noteworthy actions which gained the admiration and respect of everyone.

About this time Julius II had to deal with a delicate matter that verged on schism. At his election he had promised to convoke within two years a Council in France. Louis XII, the King of France, and Maximilian, the Emperor, tried to force the Pope to hasten the convocation of the Council. Having failed in their efforts to intimidate the Pope, they prevailed upon five Cardinals to break with Rome and to call a council of their own at Pisa. Upon the advice of Cajetan, Julius II countered by calling together a General Council of the Church. At the same time Cajetan put his men under strict orders not to join hands in any way with the schismatics. He even sent several of his best theologians to Pisa in order to organize a resistance movement against the schismatic council. Personally he engaged in the struggle by several tracts about the authority of the Pope. All this was of tremendous importance in snuffing out the threatening schism.

In 1518 the Holy See named Cajetan Legate to Germany. His mission was to interest the Emperor and the Electors in a crusade against the Turks under the patronage of Leo X and to receive the submission of Luther. On both counts his mission was a failure. Luther had made previous declarations of his willingness to submit to the Pope, but now completely abandoned such ideas. The story which followed was one of bitter wrangling, disappointments and growing revolt. Many historians claim that Cajetan was imprudent in his dealings with Luther and should have been more tolerant. Following these affairs there were still more troubles to plague the Cardinal in Germany. They were concerned with the election of a new Emperor. Cajetan attempted to show the mind of the Holy See in this matter, but in his efforts to be impartial he incurred the disfavor of both electoral parties.

At the end of the summer of 1519, Cajetan returned from Germany and was made Bishop of Gaeta. Once again the Pope, Adrian VI, sent him as Legate to Hungary, Bohemia and Poland, to unite these countries in a Crusade against the Turks. When Adrian VI died unexpectedly in 1523, his successor, Clement VII, recalled Cajetan to Rome. Unfortunately, Clement VII never learned to appreciate the intelligent advice of his Cardinal.

Thus Cajetan quietly resumed the life of study which his various duties had interrupted. Since he was not appreciated as an advisor, he sought to do good by intensive writing. His waning political importance was shown by the fact that in the sack of Rome (1527) his ransom was set at only 5000 ducats. However, it deprived the Cardinal of all he owned and forced him to beg for even sufficient clothing.

In 1534, the aging Cardinal fell sick, and on October 10th of the same year, he died. At his express command he was buried in all simplicity at the entrance to the Church of *Santa Maria sopra Minerva* in the heart of Rome.

The Works of Cajetan

In Cajetan's literary career we may distinguish three periods. The first, which runs from 1494 to 1499, is mostly devoted to philosophical writings, though not exclusively. From this period date the following philosophical works:

In de Ente et Essentia D. Thomae Aquinatis Commentaria (1495)
Commentaria in reliquum libri secundi peri Hermeneias (1496)
In libros Posteriorum Analyticorum Aristotelicos additamenta (1496)
Commentaria in Isagogen Porphyrii (1497)
Commentaria in Praedicamenta Aristotelis (1498)
De Nominum Analogia (1498)
**Commentaria in VIII libros Physicorum Aristotelis* (1498)
**Commentaria in IV libros de Coelo et Mundo Aristotelis* (1498)
**Commentaria super Metaphysicam Aristotelis* (1498)
De subjecto naturalis philosophiae (1499)

In later times only three other purely philosophical works were added to this list. They are:

Commentaria in III libros Aristotelis de Anima (1509)
De conceptu entis (1509)
Utrum detur in naturalibus potentia neutra (1510)

Of these works, those marked with an asterisk have never been published.

The second period runs from 1499 to 1523 and comprises mostly theological works. Many of them are concerned with moral issues, such as his famous *Summula Peccatorum,* others are polemical in nature and deal with the religious controversies stirred up by the Reformation. From this time also dates the most important of Cajetan's work, his immortal *Commentaria* on the *Summa Theologica* of St. Thomas (1507-1522).

The third period, from 1523-1534, produced mostly exegetical works, chiefly commentaries on the books of the Old and New Testaments. His use of the original Hebrew and Greek texts, his insistence upon the literal sense of the text, and his sharp analysis of its meaning, made him a trail blazer in contemporary Catholic exegesis, although his works are not entirely free from defects.

In none of his works did Cajetan indulge in the glittering elegance of style so beloved by his humanist contemporaries. *Res, non verba* was his guiding principle. Yet the great humanist Erasmus praised him for this love of brevity and compactness, and preferred it to the literary smoothness of others who so often did nothing but add to the confusion by a barrage of words. Sometimes this very brevity leads to a complexity of sentences which is rather puzzling, especially when the subject matter itself is one that demands considerable concentration of attention. Notwithstanding such occasional obscurities, his views are generally stated with great clarity and perspicuity. His works have earned for him one of the first places, if not the very first, among Thomistic philosophers and theologians, not only of his time, but of all times.

The de Nominum Analogia

Although Cajetan wrote his treatise *The Analogy of Names* at the youthful age of thirty, it shows no traces of the immaturity which usually reveals itself in the earlier works even of great philosophers. Without any sign of hesitation or uncertainty, he systematically explains the whole Thomistic theory of analogy in such a way that neither he himself nor any subsequent philosophers have found reason to add anything to the fundamental principles and outlines laid down by him. As John of St. Thomas confesses: "As regards difficulties in analogy which are of a rather metaphysical nature, Cajetan has discussed them so extensively and so thoroughly in his little treatise *The Analogy of Names* that he has not left us any opportunity to think out another one."[3] And Sylvester of Ferrara agrees: "As regards other difficulties which may be raised concerning the analogy of names, if you want to understand them fully, you should consult that most ingenious work, *The Analogy of Names,* written by the Most Reverend Thomas Cajetan."[4]

The *reason* which prompted Cajetan to write *The Analogy of Names* is given by him in the opening passage of the treatise itself: "Motivated both by the obscurity of the subject itself and the deplorable scarcity of profound studies in our age, I intend to publish during this vacation a treatise on the analogy of names. An understanding of this doctrine is so necessary that without it no one can study metaphysics, and ignorance of it give rise to many errors in other sciences."

Cajetan's warning is still just as appropriate nowadays as it was in the fifteenth century. Neglect of the metaphysical nature of analogy has contributed much to the decadence of scholastic philosophy in the past,[5] and ignorance of it causes many to see in Thomistic metaphysics and theology nothing but a miasmic confusion of anthropomorphic ideas. Between the extreme univocity advocated by monism and the extreme equivocity of pluralism, between anthropomorphism and complete agnosticism, there is but one middle ground—metaphysical analogy. It is this analogy which forms the main theme of Cajetan's *The Analogy of Names.* True, the name itself of this treatise may give the impression that he considers analogy primarily as a logical subject. However, as he tells us in Chapter Four, the term *names* is not to be taken as synonymous with words, i.e. as grammatico-logical elements, but comprises not only the external word and the concept in the mind, but also the reality outside the mind.[6]

The *order and form* of the treatise will be clear from a glance at the table of contents. After a brief consideration of analogy in general (nos. 1-3), Cajetan consecrates three chapters to a study of the three modes of analogy traditionally admitted, at least in practice, by his predecessors. In Chapters Four to Ten he carefully analyzes

---

[3]*Logica,* II, 13, 3 (Reiser ed. of the *Cursus Philosophicus,* vol. I, p. 481, col. 2).

[4]Comment. in *Summa Contra Gentiles,* I, 34 (XI, in Leonine ed.).

[5]Cf. G. M. Petazzi, *"Univocita od Analogia?"* in *Rivista di filosofia neoscholastica,* 1911-1912, p. 35.

[6]Chapter Four, no. 31.

the nature of analogy, especially that of so-called analogy of proper proportionality. In these chapters Cajetan usually follows the method of St. Thomas—first certain objections are proposed, then the problem is considered and finally the objections are answered. Often he adds a kind of scholion to explain some particular point not fully considered in the preceding part of the chapter. Chapter Eleven is of a more practical nature. In it, he indicates the safeguards to be taken in order to avoid errors in the use of analogous terms.

As regards the *sources* of his doctrine, Cajetan takes pain to make it clear that he is merely systematizing and developing the teachings of Aristotle, Averroes and especially St. Thomas. Continually he appeals to them, as will be clear from a glance at the Index of Names and Quotations on pages 88f. That this appeal is not mere lip-service will be clear from a careful comparison of the teachings of St. Thomas and Cajetan in the matter of analogy.[7] Hence it is not surprising that very few Thomistic philosophers subscribe to the view of Descoqs that in important points Cajetan's theory of analogy was an innovation.[8] As a faithful interpreter of St. Thomas, Cajetan supplemented something which hitherto had been lacking in the imposing structure of Thomistic philosophy—a coherent, systematic and professional study of analogy itself, rather than its applications to other philosophical and theological problems. It is a well-known fact that St. Thomas speaks about analogy almost as frequently as about act and potency or participation; yet his main concern was with the application of analogy to philosophical and theological problems. Because of the complex nature of analogy and the fact that several modes of it may be at work in the same problem, it is not surprising that many have experienced almost unsurmountable difficulties in studying analogy in St. Thomas and have even seen contradictions in his teachings. Cajatan's treatise points out the self-consistency of St. Thomas and how such difficulties and apparent contradictions may be solved. In view of all this it is not surprising that his work has been accepted as the faithful interpretation and development of the Thomistic theory of analogy by nearly all Thomistic philosophers.

---

[7]This comparison has been made by A. Goergen in his work *Kardinal Cajetans Lehre von der Analogie; ihr Verhaeltnis zu Thomas von Aquin,* Speyer, 1938.

[8]P. Descoqs, *Institutiones metaphysicae generalis,* Paris, 1924, vol. I, p. 277f.

However, there is no need to defend Cajetan against any attacks. He himself is the best defender of his own positions. Hence we shall not prolong this introduction any longer, but let Cajetan speak for himself.

CHAPTER ONE

DIVISION OF ANALOGY, ANALOGY OF INEQUALITY

Introduction

1 Motivated both by the obscurity of the subject itself and by the deplorable scarcity of profound studies in our age, I intend to publish during this vacation[1] a treatise on the analogy of names. An understanding of this doctrine is so necessary that without it no one can study metaphysics,[2] and ignorance of it gives rise to many errors in other sciences.[3] If ever at any time there was a lack of understanding of analogy, it is clearly the situation now when authors make analogy consist in unity of "indisjunction," of order, or of a prescinded concept which is unequally participated in.[4] For from the following discussions it will become clear that such theories have wandered over roads of ruin away from the truth which spontaneously manifested itself.

[1]Summer of 1498. Cf. no. 125.

[2]Cf. no. 29. Being as such, which is the formal object of metaphysics, is analogous; hence it follows that all truly metaphysical concepts will be analogous.

[3]Cf. St. Thomas, in *Boethium de Trinitate,* q. 6, a. 2: "Errors are committed by those who try to proceed in a uniform way in the three branches of speculative science," i.e. in physics, mathematics and metaphysics. As examples of errors resulting from the neglect of analogy in "other sciences" we may point to theologians who conceive creation anthropomorphically as a kind of generation, and to scientists who conceive all causality after the manner of mechanical causes. For a detailed examination as to how neglect of analogy led to errors in the philosophy of nature, see Andrew G. van Melsen, *The Philosophy of Nature,* Pittsburgh, 1953, Ch. IV, Sections 5-7 and Ch. V, Section 3.

[4]The Latin has: *dum analogiam vel indisiunctionis, vel ordinis, vel conceptus praecisi unitate, cum inaequalis participatione constituunt.* There is a parallel passage in Ch. VI, no. 71: *patent quod analogum non conceptum disjunctum, nec unum praecisum inaequaliter participatum, nec unum ordine, sed conceptum unum proportione dicit et praedicat.* (It is evident that an analogous term does not express and predicate a disjunct concept, nor a concept which is one by precision and unequally participated in, nor a concept which is one by order, but a concept which is one by proportion.) In this text *"disjunct concept"* refers to concepts such as that of the dogfish and the ordinary dog, mentioned in no. 63, i.e. concepts expressed by an equivocal or "indisjunct" term; *"a concept which is one by precision and unequally participated in"* refers to the concept of animality as realized in man, ox and lion, mentioned in no. 64, i.e. to analogy of inequality; the *"concept which is one by order"* is not specifically mentioned in Ch. VI, but in Ch. V, nos. 51-52, Cajetan speaks of the unity of order found in analogy of attribution. In the present text *"indisjunction"* may therefore be understood as referring to diverse concepts expressed by an "indisjunct" term or the confusion of

Division

2 In this work the word *analogy* means proportion or proportionality, as we have learned from the Greeks.[5] However, the term has been subjected to so many extensions and distinctions that many names are erroneously spoken of as analogous, and confusion would result from any effort to reconcile these many distinctions. However, lest we neglect the main issue through an investigation of what is only of secondary importance, and be accused of using a peculiar terminology, we shall include all the variations under one threefold division, and we shall proceed from those terms which are less properly analogous to those which are truly analogous.

3 All analogous terms can be reduced to three modes[6] of analogy:

Analogy of Inequality
Analogy of Attribution
Analogy of Proportionality.[7]

---

analogy with equivocation; *"order"* refers to analogy based upon relationship or order, which, according to Cajetan, is called analogy only in an incorrect sense (cf. no. 23), or perhaps to analogy according to genus (analogy of inequality), "which admits within itself many natures ordered to one another" (no. 5); *"a concept which is one by precision and unequally participated in"* refers to analogy of inequity (cf. nos. 4-7).

[5]Analogia (*analogía*) originated as a mathematical term indicating equality of ratios (Euclid, VII Df. 20). Plato (*Republic,* 534a6) and Aristotle (*Physics,* VII, 4; 249a, 24) introduced the term into philosophy to indicate proportions which are not mathematical.

[6]The Zammit edition of 1934 and the Zammit-Hering edition of 1952 refer in a footnote to the modes of analogy as *"species of analogy."* Taken in its proper sense, the term *species* would indicate that this division of analogy is a division of a genus into species; hence analogy itself would be a univocal concept. Analogy itself, however, is not univocal but analogous. As St. Thomas warns, "the univocal is divided according to differences, but the analogous according to diverse modes." (In *I Sentent.* 22, 1, 3, *ad* 2; see also *de Potentia* 9, 3 *ad* 6). Catejan does not speak of *species of* analogy but of *modes* of analogy and thus safeguards the analogous character of analogy itself.

[7]Aristotle mentions these three modes of analogy, although he does not call them by the names given by Catejan. *Analogy of inequality* is mentioned in Physics VII, 4 (249a 22ff.): "This discussion serves to show that the genus is not a unity but contains a plurality latent in it and distinct from it, and that in the case of equivocal terms sometimes the different senses in which they are used are far removed from one another, while sometimes there is a certain likeness between them, and sometimes again they are nearly related either generically or analogically, with the result that they seem not to be equivocal though they really are." *Analogy of attribution* is mentioned in *Nic. Ethics* I., 6 (1096b 26ff.): "But what then do we mean by the good? Are goods one, then, by being derived from one good or by all contributing to one good, or are they rather one by analogy?" *Analogy of proportionality* is mentioned in *Topics* I, 17 (108a 6ff.): "Likeness should be studied,

However, according to the true sense of the term[8] and the practice of Aristotle,[9] only the last mode constitutes analogy, and the first one is entirely foreign to analogy.[10]

Analogy of Inequality

4 *Its Nature.* Things are said to be analogous by analogy of inequality if they have a common name, and the notion indicated by this name is exactly the same but unequally participated in. We are speaking here of inequality of perfection; for example, *body* is a term common to inferior and superior bodies,[11] and the notion of all bodies, insofar as they are bodies, is the same. If the question is asked, What is fire[12] insofar as it is a body? the answer will be: a substance subject to the three dimensions; and likewise to the question, What is the heaven insofar as it is a body? etc. Nevertheless the notion of corporeity is not in inferior and superior bodies according to an equal grade of perfection.

5 *Its Names.* The logician refers to analogous terms of this type as univocal. The philosopher, on the other hand, regards them as equivocal, the difference coming from the fact that the former considers the intentions expressed by the names, and the latter their

---

first, in the case of things belonging to different genera, the formulae being 'A : B = C : D' (e g. as knowledge stands to the object of knowledge, so is sensation to the object of sensation), and 'As A is to B, so is C to D' e.g. as sight is in the eye, so is reason in the soul, and as is a calm in the sea, so is windlessness in the air)."

St. Thomas refers to them in the well-known text in *I Sentent.* 19, 5, 2, *ad* 1 quoted below in footnote 16 of Chapter One.

[8]The Greek prefix *anà* expresses comparison, relationship or repetition; *lógos* means idea or term expressing an idea; hence etymologically, *analogía* or analogy is taken to mean the mutual relationship or proportion of ideas or terms. If something is spoken of "according to analogy" (*kat'analogían*), the meaning is "according to a mutual relationship of ideas or terms," i.e. according to proportionality.

[9]Cf. *Nic. Ethics* I, 6 (1096b, 26ff.), quoted above in footnote 7.

[10]Cf. No. 7.

[11]According to ancient physics, there is a hierarchy of bodies in the universe; superior or celestial bodies begin with the sphere of the moon, the first of the celestial bodies. Cf. J. de Tonquedec, *Questions de Cosmologie et de Physique chez Aristote et Saint Thomas,* Paris, 1950, p. 16.

[12]According to ancient physics fire was a separate sphere of the universe and a kind of body unable to be seen by the senses. In one way or another it entered into the composition of other bodies. Cf. J. de Tonquedec, *op. cit.* pp. 14f.

natures.[13] That is why Aristotle in *X Metaphysics*[14] states that the corruptible and the incorruptible have nothing in common which is univocal, because he scorns unity which is merely unity of reason or concept. And in *VII Physics*[15] we are told that in analogy according to genus equivocations lie hidden because analogy of this type with its unity of concept does not simply imply one nature, but admits within itself many natures that are ordered to one another, as is clear with respect to the species of any genus, and especially the most special and subaltern species. For every genus can be called analogous in this way, as is clear from quantity and quality in the predicaments, and body, etc., although it is not a general custom to do so except for the most general genera and those close to them.

6 *St. Thomas,* in *I Sentent.* dist. 19, refers to this type of analogy as analogy *"according to 'to be' only,"*[16] because the analogates are

---

[13]Cf. St. Thomas, *in VII Physics,* lect. 8 (Leonine edition, no. 8): "The name *body,* as applied to a celestial body and a corruptible body, is used equivocally from the viewpoint of a student of nature because their matter is not the same. Nevertheless, they agree in a logical genus and because of this generic agreement they do not at all seem to be equivocal." Cf. also *in I Sentent.* 19, 5, 2, *ad* 1, quoted in footnote 16.

[14]Ch. 10 (1059a 7ff.): "The characteristics, then, in respect of which and in direct consequence of which one thing is perishable and another imperishable, are opposite, so that the things must be considered to be different in kind."

[15]Ch. 4 (249a 22ff.), quoted above in footnote 7.

[16]Q.5, a. 2, *ad* 1: "There are three ways in which something may be said by analogy. [In the first place,] according to intention only and not according to 'to be.' This happens when one intention refers to several things according to priority and posteriority, but has a 'to be' in one only. For example, the intention *health* refers to animal, urine and diet, in a different manner according to priority and posteriority, but not according to a diversity of 'to be,' because health has a 'to be' only in animals.

[In the second place,] according to 'to be' and not according to intention. This happens when several are considered equal in the intention of something they have in common, but this common element does not have a 'to be' of the same kind in all. For example, all bodies are considered equally in the intention of *corporeity.* Hence the logician, who considers only intentions, says that the name *body* is predicated univocally of all bodies. However, the 'to be' of this nature is not of the same character in corruptible and incorruptible bodies. Hence for the metaphysicist and the philosopher of nature, who consider things according to their 'to be,' neither the name *body* nor any other name is predicated univocally of corruptible and incorruptible bodies, as is clear from the Philosopher and the Commentator in *X Metaphysics* [Ch. 10 (1059a 7ff.)].

[In the third place,] according to intention and according to 'to be.' This happens when a thing is considered neither equal in a common intention nor equal in 'to be.' For example, *being* is predicated of substance and accident in this way. In such cases the common nature must have a 'to be' in each of those things of which it is predicated, but this 'to be' differs according to a higher or a lesser degree of perfection. In this manner I say that truth, goodness and all other similar terms are predicated of God and creatures by analogy."

considered equal in the formality signified by the common name but are not held equal with respect to the 'to be' of this common formality. For the formality of every genus has a more perfect 'to be' in one thing than in another, as we see so often in metaphysics. For instance, not only is a plant more noble than a mineral, but corporeity is more noble in a plant than in a mineral; and the same goes for other perfections.

7 *Averroes,* too, in *XII Metaphysics,*[17] bears witness to this type of analogy, saying that notwithstanding the unity of the genus there remains priority and posteriority[18] among those things that are included in the genus. They are called analogous only insofar as, in consideration of the unequal perfection of the inferiors, the common name is predicated of them according to priority and posteriority in the order of perfection. This way of speaking already has become an accepted custom, so that it is deemed synonymous for something to be predicated analogically or according to priority and posteriority.

Conclusion. Nevertheless, this is a misuse[19] of the terms; for to speak of something according to priority and posteriority is broader than speaking analogically.[20] In analogous terms of this sort there

[17]"Priority is found in the same genus and in diverse genera which are spoken of with respect to the same thing; as e.g. being is spoken of with respect to the ten predicaments." (ed. Venet., apud Juntas, 1552, vol. VIII, fol. 137, 22-23).

[18]Concerning these terms, see below, footnote 8 of Chapter Nine.

[19]Cajetan's insistance that analogy of inequality and of attribution are called analogies only by a misuse of language (cf. nos. 3, 21, 23), may be explained by his dismay about the ignorance of true metaphysical analogy. However, he does not reject them absolutely, as is clear from no. 2, where he calls them analogy "in a less proper sense." Cf. also John of St. Thomas, *Logica,* II, 13, 3 (in Reiser ed. of the *Cursus Philos.* I, p. 485). As Ramirez remarks, "Although analogy according to 'to be' only is usually neglected by the later scholastics, nevertheless Aristotle and St. Thomas frequently made use of it, and justly so, for the metaphysicist and the theologian, who consider the 'to be' of things, must pay careful attention to the grades and order of being of existing reality." *De analogia secundum doctrinam Aristotelico-Thomisticam,* Madrid, 1921, p. 53.

[20]In his commentary on *de Ente et Essentia, cap.* 2 (q. 3, nos. 17 and 18 in Laurent edition), Cajetan writes: "The question may be raised whether *being* is predicated by priority of substance and by posteriority of accident or univocally of both . . . In two ways something may be predicated of several by priority and posteriority. In one way, according to the 'to be' of this predicate, and in another, according to the proper notion of the same. *By analogy according to 'to be'* is said to be predicated that which has a more perfect 'to be' in one than in another. In this way every genus is predicated of its species by priority and posteriority because it must necessarily have a more perfect 'to be' in one species than in another. For this reason the Commentator [in *XII Metaphysics,* ed. Venet., 1552, vol. 8, fol. 137r-v] says that priority and posteriority of species does not prevent generic unity. Presently, however,

is no need to determine their position as regards unity, abstraction, predication, comparison, demonstration, etc.; for as a matter of fact they are univocal, and therefore the rules of univocal terms must be observed with respect to them.

---

we are not concerned [with this manner of predication according to priority and posteriority] for it is self-evident to anyone that being is in substance in a more perfect way than in accidents and that in this way it is predicated by priority and posteriority.

Analogously, i.e. by priority and posteriority *with respect to its proper notion,* is said to be predicated that which is predicated of one without a respect to another, but of the other only with respect to the first. For instance, *healthy* is predicated of animal independently from a respect to diet, medicine and urine, but of these things it is predicated only with respect to animal . . . For you will say . . . that urine is healthy because it is a sign of health, a diet because it preserves health, and medicine because it causes health. In this way a doubt is raised whether *being* is predicated analogously, in the sense of being predicated of substance absolutely and of accidents only relatively to substance. This question amounts to the same as asking whether substance insofar as it is a being does not include accident, and accident insofar as it is a being includes substance."

CHAPTER TWO

ANALOGY OF ATTRIBUTION

Definition

8 Analogous by attribution are those things which have a common name, and the notion signified by this name is the same with respect to the term but different as regards the relationships to this term. For example, the name *healthy* is common to medicine, urine and animal, but the notion of all insofar as healthy expresses different relationships to one term, namely, health. For if anyone describes what an animal is insofar as it is healthy, he will say that it is the subject of health, and that urine insofar as it is healthy is a sign of health, whereas medicine insofar as it is healthy will be mentioned as a cause of health. In this example it is perfectly clear that the notion of health is not entirely the same nor entirely different, but to a certain extent the same and to a certain extent different. For there is a diversity of relationships, but the term of those relationships is one and the same.

Division

9 This type of analogy can come about in four ways, according to the four genera of causes (we will for the moment call the exemplary cause the formal cause). With respect to some one denomination and attribution, it may happen that several things are related differently to one end, one efficient cause, one exemplar, and one subject, as is clear from the examples of Aristotle in *IV Metaphysics*.[1] The example of *healthy* in *III Metaphysics*[2] refers to the final cause, the example of *medical*,[3] in the same text, pertains to the efficient cause,

[1]Ch. 2 (1003a 32-1003b 15).

[2]"Everything which is healthy is related to health, one thing in the sense that it preserves health, another in the sense that it produces it, another in the sense that it is a symptom of health, another because it is capable of it." *Metaphysics* IV, 2 (1003a 34ff.). Cf. *Topics* I, 15 (106b 34ff. and 107b 34ff.), and St. Thomas, in *IV Metaphysics*, lect. 1, no. 537.

[3]"And that which is medical is relative to the medical art, one thing being called medical because it possesses it, another because it is naturally adapted to it, another because it is a function of the medical art." *Metaphysics* IV, 2 (1003b 1ff.). Cf. St. Thomas, in *IV Metaphysics*, lect. 1, no. 538; in *XI Metaphysics*, lect. 3, no. 2196; *de Principiis Naturae* (in the critical text edited by John J. Pauson, Louvain 1950, Ch. 6, p. 103, and in the translation of R. J. Henle and V. J. Bourke, St. Louis, 1947, pp. 83ff.).

the analogy of *being*[4] (likewise mentioned in the same text) pertains to the material cause, and finally the analogy of *good,* given in *I Ethics*[5] refers to the exemplary cause.

Conditions

10 Many conditions are attached to this analogy. They follow one another in an orderly fashion.

First Condition. This analogy is according to extrinsic denomination only, so that only the primary analogate realizes the perfection formally,[6] whereas the others have it only by extrinsic denomination.[7]

---

[4]"So, too, there are many senses in which a thing is said to be, but all refer to one starting point; some things are said to be because they are substances, others because they are affections of substance or destructions or privations or qualities of substance, or of things related to substance or productive or generative of substance or of things which are relative to substance, or negations of one of these things or substance itself. "*Metaphysics* IV, 2 (1003b 5ff.)." Cf. St. Thomas in *IV Metaphysics,* lect. 1, no. 539.

[5]*Nic. Ethics* I, 6 (1096b 26ff.), quoted above in footnote 7 of Chapter One. For its context the whole chapter should be read. Cf. also *Topics* IV,2 (123b 8ff.), and St. Thomas in *I Ethics,* lect. 7, no. 93ff. (Spiazzi or Pirotta edition).

[6]Cf. Cajetan's commentary in *S. T.* I, 16, 6 (VI, in Leonine edition), where he says: "To be in one only according to its proper nature is a condition of names which are *to one* or *from one* etc., but not of names predicated proportionally."

[7]Cf. Cajetan's commentary in *S. T.* I, 6, 4 (III-VIII), where he says: "Denomination is twofold. One is intrinsic and the other extrinsic. A denomination is called *intrinsic* when the form of the denominative [perfection] is in that which is denominated, say, white, quantified, etc.; whereas a denomination is *extrinsic* if the form of the denominative [perfection] is not in the denominated thing; e.g., located, measured and the like. All agree that there can be extrinsic denomination according to names implying relationship, as is exemplified by *located* and *measured.* But Plato and Aristotle differ as to whether or not there can be extrinsic denomination according to names implying something absolute. This difference concerns us because *good* is an absolute name, and the divine goodness is extrinsic to things."

(VIII)"In two ways a thing may be called such or such after something extrinsic. In one way, if the reason for the denomination is the very *relationship* [of this thing] to something extrinsic; e.g., urine is called healthy for the sole reason of its relationship as a sign of health. In another way, if the reason for the denomination is not a relationship of similitude or any other, but a form which is the *foundation of a relationship* of similitude to an extrinsic thing; e.g., air is said to be lucid because of the light of the sun inasmuch as it participates in it through the form of light.

When a denomination is made in the first way, there is a purely extrinsic denomination, but when the denomination is made in the second way, there is extrinsic denomination, yet not only extrinsic denomination because there is also intrinsic denomination, as is clear. This happens in the case under consideration [the goodness of creatures]. Hence the text says that all things are called good by way of assimilation. And from this it follows immediately that they can be called *good* both by extrinsic and by intrinsic denomination . . .

As has been touched upon already, extrinsic denomination is twofold. It is *pure* if the denomination is made solely because of the relationship to the

For example, the animal itself is called *healthy* formally, whereas urine, medicine and other similar things are called healthy not because of health inherent to them, but extrinsically after the health of the animal, insofar as they signify it, cause it, or have some other relationship to it. The same goes for *medical* and for *substance,* which are formally in the primary analogate, but with respect to the other analogates they are spoken of in denominative signification and extrinsically.[8] The notion of *good,* also, which is verified in the essential good, and after which the others are denominated good in the order of exemplarity, is realized formally only in the first good; the others are called good by extrinsic denomination and in relation to the first good.

11 It should be carefully noted that this first condition of this mode of analogy, namely, that it is not according to the genus of inherent formal causality, but always according to something extrinsic, must be understood formally and not materially. It should not be understood as if every name which is analogous by analogy of attribution is common to the analogates in such a way that it pertains only to the primary analogate formally and to the others by extrinsic denomination, as happens to be the case with *healthy* and *medical.* Such a generalization is false, as is clear from *being*[9] and *good,* and cannot be gathered from what we have said unless it were understood ma-

---

denominating form. It is *causal* if the participation of the effect in the extrinsic cause is the foundation of the denomination. For this reason, in the present question [everything] is called [good by the divine goodness] *as its principle* because everything is said to be good extrinsically by the divine goodness, not in just any way but causally. If one considers this [explanation] carefully, he will find that with respect to absolute names a purely extrinsic denomination is impossible, although a causal denomination can be made."

[8]The text of the Parisian edition of 1511 is clearer. It has: "*Medical,* also, which is derived from the medical art, formally denominates the physician. But the instrument and whatever else is called medical is spoken of by extrinsic denomination after this art. Substance, too, which is the subject of 'to be' and its possessor, alone is called a *being* in a formal sense; other things are called beings because they are measures, dispositions, active [principles], etc. of this being." Cf. the text of Aristotle quoted in footnote 4.

[9]Cf. Cajetan's commentary in *S. T.* I, 13, 5 (XIV): "*Being* is not analogous to God and creatures according to extrinsic denomination as *healthy* is. But there is a similarity insofar as in both cases there is analogy because of the order of two things to one another, although [this analogy] is found in a dissimilar way in one and the other. Between God and creature there is a formal similitude of imitation, whereas between a healthy animal and urine there is no similitude but a relationship of signification. Hence in the first case there is an analogous community according to formal predication, whereas in the second, properly speaking, there is a community of attribution to one according to any kind of predication, whether intrinsic or extrinsic, etc.

terially.[10] Our explanation must be understood in the sense that every name which is analogous by attribution as such, i.e. insofar as it is analogous in this manner, is common to the analogates in this way that it pertains to the primary analogate formally and to the others by extrinsic denomination.

This assertion is, indeed, true if the preceding explanation is understood formally, and clearly follows from it. For although *being* agrees formally with all substances, accidents, etc., nevertheless insofar as all are denominated from being taken subjectively as such, substance alone is being formally, and the others are called beings because they are qualities, activities, etc. of being. However, under a different aspect they could be called beings in a formal sense.

The same applies to *good*. Although all beings are good by goodnesses formally inherent in them, nevertheless when they are called good with respect to the first goodness considered as their efficient, final, or exemplary cause, all other things are said to be good by a purely extrinsic denomination—namely, by that goodness by which God Himself is formally good.

12 *Second Condition.* Another condition follows immediately from the first—the one thing which is the term of the diverse relationships in analogous names of this type is *one* not merely in concept but numerically.[11] This assertion can be understood in two manners according as the analogates themselves can be taken in two ways, viz. universally and particularly.

---

[10]Cf. St. Thomas in *de Veritate* 21, 4, *ad* 2: "In two manners a thing is denominated in relation to another. In one way, when the *relation* itself is the reason of the denomination. For example, urine is said to be healthy in relation to the health of the animal, for the notion *healthy* as predicated of urine is a sign of the animal's health. In such cases, what is denominated in relation to another is not denominated from some form inherent to it, but from something extrinsic to which it is referred. In another way, something is denominated in relation to another when not the relation but its *cause* is the reason of the denomination. For example, air is said to be lucid from the sun, not because the reference itself of the air to the sun is the lucidity of the air, but because the direct opposition of the air to the sun is the cause of its lucidity." Concerning St. Thomas' theory of light, see J. de Tonquedec, *op. cit.*, pp. 74ff.

[11]Cf. St. Thomas, in *IV Metaphysics,* lect. 1, no. 536: "It is to be noted that the *one* to which the diverse relations refer in analogous names, is *one* numerically and not only in concept as is the case with the one indicated by a univocal name. For this reason [Aristotle] says that, although being is predicated in many ways, it is not predicated equivocally but by reference to some one thing, not indeed to some one thing which is one in concept only, but which is one as some one nature." Cf. also *ibidem,* nos. 537-539; and *S. T.* I-II, 20, 3, *ad* 3.

If the analogates are taken *particularly,* the single term is necessarily one in number truly and positively. If, however, they are taken *universally,* the single term is necessarily one in number negatively, i.e. it is not multiplied numerically in the analogates as a universal, although in itself it is something universal and not numerically one. For example, if we consider this healthy urine, this healthy medicine, and this healthy animal, all are called healthy with respect to the health that is in this animal which, of course, is truly numerically one. Socrates,[12] for instance, is said to be healthy because he has this health, medicine because it causes this health, and urine because it signifies this same health, etc.

If, however, we consider healthy animal, healthy urine and healthy medicine in a general way, the health by which these three are called healthy, formally speaking, is not in itself numerically one, because universal causes must be assigned to universal effects, as is said in *II Physics.*[13] The same goes for the signs, instruments, preservatives, and other things of this sort—*healthy* is numerically one in these analogates in a negative way. For health is not multiplied numerically in animal, urine and diet, since there is not one health in urine, another in animal, and a third in diet.

13 This second condition follows from the first. For what is common by extrinsic denomination does not multiply its denominator in the denominated in the same way as a univocal term is multiplied in its univocates. Because of its manner of multiplication a univocal name is said to be one in concept only and not numerically one in its univocates. For instance, there is one animality in man, another in a horse, and another in an ox, but they are all united in one concept under the name *animal.*

14 *Third Condition.* From the above condition a third can be derived —the primary analogate is put into the definition of the others with respect to the analogous name.[14] The reason is that the other analogates

---

[12]The text has *Sortes* instead of *Socrates.*

[13]Ch. 3 (195b 25ff.): "Generic effects must be assigned to generic causes, particular effects to particular causes, e.g., statue to sculptor, this statue to this sculptor."

[14]Cf. St. Thomas, *S. T.* I, 13, 6: "In names predicated of many in an analogous sense, all must be predicated through a respect to some one thing, and this one thing must be put into the definition of all. And since the essence signified by the name is the definition, as Aristotle says [*Metaphysics* IV, 7 (1012a 23)], it is necessary that such a name be predicated primarily of that which is put into the definition of other things, and secondarily of the

do not have this name predicated of them except by attribution in relation to the primary analogate, in which the perfection expressed by it is formally realized. For instance, the health of animal is included in the notion of medicine, diet, urine, etc., insofar as they are healthy; and without the health of animal they cannot be understood to be healthy. The same goes for the other examples of analogous terms.

15 *Fourth Condition.* From the preceding it follows further that a name which is analogous in this manner does not have one definite meaning common to all its partial modes, i.e., to all its analogates. Consequently, it does not have an objective concept nor a formal concept which abstracts from the concepts of the analogates. The only thing in common is the external word which implies an identical term diversely referred to. Accordingly, in this type of analogy there are three elements—the external word, the term, and diverse relationships to this term. The analogous name signifies the term distinctly; e.g., healthy distinctly signifies health. The diverse relationships, however, are implied in such an indeterminate and confused way that the primary relationship is signified distinctly or almost distinctly, but the others in a confused[15] manner and by way of reduction to the primary relationship.

For instance, in one word which distinctly implies health, *healthy* renders confusedly many relationships to health, e.g. possessing it, manifesting it, causing it, etc. It does this in such a way that it distinctly signifies the primary relationship (that of being the possessor or subject of health; for we predicate healthy absolutely of whatever has health as its subject); whereas the other relationships are implied indeterminately and by attribution with respect to the primary analogate, as is evident from what has been said above.

16 *Conclusion.* Therefore, concerning an analogous term of this type three assertions can be made—1) it is common to all the analogates not merely as regards the external word; 2) if used absolutely, it

---

others according as they approach more or less to the first. For instance, *healthy* which is predicated of the animal body is put into the definition of healthy as predicated of medicine, which is called healthy inasmuch as it causes health in the animal, and also in the definition of healthy as predicated of urine, which is called healthy inasmuch as it is a sign of health in the animal."

[15]In Cajetan's language the verb *to confuse* and its derivatives should be understood in the original sense of con-fusing or implying indeterminately.

stands for the primary analogate;[16] 3) there is nothing prior to the primary analogate in which the whole perfection expressed by the analogous term is formally realized. The analogous term, indeed, signifies the primary analogate in a more special way and does not possess a meaning which transcends all the analogates.

Its Division by St. Thomas

17 This analogy is divided by St. Thomas[17] into analogy of *two to a third,* such as of urine and medicine to a healthy animal, and analogy of *one to another,* such as of urine or medicine to a healthy animal.

18 This division does not add any new members to those given above [in no. 9] because it embraces analogy according to all the genera of causes.[18] It is made in order to show that the analogous term is taken in a different way when, on the one hand, the primary analogate is posited as one extreme and the other analogates as the other, and when, on the other hand, one of the secondary analogates is posited as one extreme and the other as the other extreme, no matter according to what genus of causality the analogy arises. For to the primary and the other analogates the analogous term is common in such a way that it does not posit or signify anything prior to them, and for this reason it is called *analogy of one to another,* everything different from the primary analogate being identified with the *one.* To the secondary analogates, however, the analogous term is common in such a way that it posits something prior to them all—namely, the first term in relation to which all others are spoken of by attribution. In this case it is called *analogy of two to a third* or *of many to one*[19] because it is not in relation to one another but in relation to the primary analogate that there is attribution.[20]

[16]Cf. St. Thomas, *S. T.* II-II, 186, 1: "What belongs to many in common is attributed by way of antonomasia to that to which it belongs *par excellence.*"

[17]Cf. *de Potentia* 7, 7: "This [analogous] predication can occur in two ways. In one way, something is predicated *of two* because of a relation *to a third;* e.g., as *being* is predicated of quality and quantity in relation to substance. In another way, something is predicated of two because of the relation of *one to the other,* as *being* is predicated of substance and quantity." Cf. also *Contra Gentes* I, 34, *de Veritate* 2, 11, *ad* 6 and *S. T.* I, 13, 5.

[18]Concerning the relationship of this division to that according to the four genera of causes (no. 9), cf. Penido, *op. cit.* pp. 28-36.

[19]Cf. St. Thomas, *Contra Gentes* I, 34.

[20]Cf. Cajetan's commentary in *S. T.* I, 13, 5 (XIII): "The meaning of *one to another* is explained by the distinction of the analogy of names—either there is analogy because of a proportion of several to one another, and this

Its Names

19 The logician calls analogous names of this type equivocal, as is clear from the beginning of the *Predicaments,*[21] where *animal* is said to be equivocal with respect to a true animal and a painting of one.[22] For the painting of an animal is not called an animal in a purely equivocal sense, but by attribution to a real animal. And it is certainly evident that in the notion of a painting of an animal insofar as it is an animal, a real animal is understood. For to the question, What is the painting of an animal insofar as it is an animal? the answer will be, an image of a real animal.[23]

20 The Greek philosophers say also that expressions *from one, in one* and *to one* lie midway between equivocal and univocal terms, as

---

analogy is called *of one to another,* or there is analogy because of a proportion of several, not to one another, but to a third, and this analogy is called *of two to a third* or *of many to one.*"

[21]*Categories* 1 (1a 1ff.): "Things are said to be named 'equivocally' when, though they have a common name, the definition corresponding with the name differs for each. Thus a real man and a figure in a picture can both lay claim to the name 'animal'; yet these are equivocally so named, for, though they have a common name, the definition corresponding with the name differs in each. For should anyone define in what sense each is an animal, his definition in the one case will be appropriate to that case only." Cajetan remarks in his commentary in *S. T.* I, 13, 5 (XII): "Analogous names are included in the equivocal names defined in the *Predicaments.* For equivocals are found in two ways. Some of them have a common name, but the notion signified by this name is totally diverse. They are called purely equivocal . . . Others have a common name, and the notion signified by this name is diverse to a certain extent. They occur in many ways and comprise also analogous names."

[22]Cf. St. Thomas, *S. T.* I, 13, 10, *ad* 3: "Animal as predicated of a real animal and a painting of one is not predicated in a purely equivocal sense, but the Philosopher uses the term *equivocal* in a broad sense so as to include analogous names, because *being,* too, which is predicated analogously, is sometimes said to be predicated equivocally of diverse predicaments." Cf. *S. T.* I, 52, 1 and *de Veritate* 14, 9, *ad* 4.

However, according to Sylvester of Ferrara in I *Contra Gentes, C.* 34 (Leonine ed. no. XII, 2): "Analogy *of one to another,* as distinguished from analogy *of two to a third,* is taken as a common name and divided into analogy of proportion and analogy of proportionality."

[23]Cf. Cajetan's commentary on the *Categories*: "A real man and a painting of a man are not given the name *animal* by pure equivocation, but by intentional equivocation or analogously, as is clear from their notions with respect to the name *animal.* These notions are not entirely diverse, but to a certain extent the same. For to the question, What is a man insofar as he is an animal? the answer is that he is a sentient animated substance, and to the question, What is the painting of a man insofar as it is an animal? the answer is that it is an image of a sentient animated substance. Hence it is clear that these notions are not entirely diverse but [only] to a certain extent." *Comment. ad Praedicamenta Aristotelis,* edit. Venet., 1506, fol. 17v, col. 1.

is evident from several texts of *Metaphysics*.[24] Moreover, in *I Ethics*[25] names of this sort are explicitly distinguished from those which are analogous, as we shall see more in detail later on.[26] The Latin pholosophers, however, call them *analogous* or *equivocal by design.*

21 St. Thomas,[27] in *I Sentent.* dist. 19, q.5, a.2, *ad* 1, refers to this analogy as analogy *"according to intention and not according to 'to be',"* because in this case the analogous term is not common according to "to be," i.e. formally, but according to intention, i.e. according to denomination. For, as is evident from the foregoing, in this analogy the common name is not realized formally except in the primary analogate and is predicated of the others by extrinsic denomination. Such names are referred to as analogous by the Latin philosophers because they imply different "proportions" to one term, the word *proportion* being used in a wide sense so as to include any relationship.[28] However, this way of speaking is incorrect, although far less than the first.[29]

Concluding Remarks

22 From the foregoing as well as from the practice of Aristotle,[30] it is easy to see how there can be scientific knowledge of this kind of analogous terms, and how they should be used to arrive at contradictions, demonstrations, conclusions, etc. First of all the diverse significations of such terms must be distinguished (for this reason the Arabs[31] called them *ambiguous* terms), and then one may proceed from the primary analogate to the others, just as from a center one can go to the circumference by various ways.

---

[24]Cf. *Metaphysics* IV, 2 (1003a 33ff.) and XI, 3 (1060b 31ff.). Also St. Thomas commentaries in *IV Metaphysics,* lect. 1, no. 535f. and in *XI Metaphysics,* lect. 3, no. 2197.

[25]*Nic. Ethics* I, 6 (1096b 26ff.), quoted in footnote 7 of Chapter One.

[26]Cf. below, no. 28.

[27]See text quoted in full in footnote 16 of Chapter One.

[28]Cf. footnotes 5 and 8 of Chapter One.

[29]Cf. footnote 18 of Chapter One.

[30]Cf., for example, *Metaphysics* IV, 2 and XI, 3.

[31]Averroes in *I Ethic.* c. VI, edit. Venet apud Juntas, 1550, vol. III, fol. 4, 21-39. Quoted below in footnote 13 of Chapter Three. Cajetan himself uses the term *ambiguous* as synonymous with *analogous* in his commentary on Porphyry's *Isagoge* (Rome, 1934, ch. I, p. 53) : "Concerning this passage the question may be raised whether being is univocal, common only in name, or ambiguous, i.e. analogous, etc. However, if a careful study has to be made, such questions go beyond the confines of logic and therefore may be postponed till we reach metaphysics."

CHAPTER THREE

ANALOGY OF PROPORTIONALITY

Nature of Analogy of Proportionality

23 *Description.* Passing over from what is called incorrectly analogous[1] to analogy in the proper sense, we say that analogous by proportionality[2] are called those things which have a common name,

[1]Cf. footnote 18 of Chapter One. In his commentary on *S. T.* I, 16, 6 (VI), he again says that "names which are *to one, in one* or *from one*" must be considered to be called "analogous incorrectly." And in his commentary on *S. T.* III, 60, 1 (II), explaining that the name *sacrament* is manifold, he repeats: "This matter is sufficiently clear from the general rules for manifold names *to one, in one* or *from one,* which incorrectly are called analogous. Whence also the author [St. Thomas] at the end of the answer to the third objection corrects this misuse of the term and after saying *analogously* immediately declares what he means, by adding 'i.e. according to a diverse relationship to one,' etc."

[2]According to P. Descoqs (*Institutiones Methaphysicae Generalis,* Paris, 1925, p. 227f.), analogy of proportionality owes its importance to Cajetan. However, St. Thomas speaks about it repeatedly. To quote only a few texts, in *I Ethics,* lect. 7, no. 95-96, he says: "In another way, one name is predicated of many according to notions which are not entirely diverse but agree in some one point. Sometimes [they agree] in this that they refer to one principle . . . Sometimes in this that they refer to one end . . . Sometimes according to diverse proportions to one subject . . . or according to one proportion to diverse subjects . . . (96) Thus [the Philosopher] says that *good* is not predicated of many according to entirely diverse notions, . . . but rather according to analogy, i.e. according to the same proportion, insofar as all good things depend upon one first principle of goodness or are ordered to one end . . . Or also all things are called good according to analogy, i.e. according to the same proportion, as sight is a good of the body and the intellect of the soul. Hence he prefers this third mode because it is taken according to goodness inherent to things, whereas the first two modes are according to separate goodness, by which a thing is denominated [good] in a less proper sense." And in *de Veritate* 2, 11 he says: "Agreement according to proportion may be twofold and thus there is a twofold community of analogy to be considered. There is some agreement between those things which have a *proportion to one another* because they are at a determined distance from one another or have some other relationship to one another . . . Sometimes, however, there is a mutual agreement of things between which there is no proportion, but rather a *similitude of two proportions;* e.g. six agrees with 4 insofar as it is twice three, just as four is twice two. The first agreement, therefore, is of *proportion,* the second of *proportionality.* Hence we find that by agreement of the first mode something is predicated of two things which are related to one another . . . Sometimes, however, something is predicated analogously according to the second mode of agreement . . . Since in analogous predication of the first mode there must be a determined relationship between the things which have something in common, it is impossible for anything to be predicated of God and creature by this mode of analogy . . . In the other mode of analogy, however, no determined relationship is found between the things that have something in common by analogy; hence there is nothing to prevent a name from being predicated of

and the notion expressed by this name is proportionally the same. Or to say the same in a different way, analogous by proportionality are called those things which have a common name, and the notion expressed by this name is similar according to a proportion.[2a] For instance, to see by corporeal vision and by intellectual vision are indicated by the common term *to see,* because just as *to understand* presents something to the mind, so *to see* presents something to the animated body.

24 *Proportion and Proportionality.* The name *proportion* is given to a definite relation of one quantity to another; e.g. we say that four is twice as much in proportion to two.[3] The name *proportionality* is given to a similitude of two proportions;[4] e.g. we say that eight is to four as six is to three, because both are twice as much in proportion, etc. However, philosophers[5] have transferred the term *proportion* [from the sphere of mathematics and use it] to express any relationship of conformity, commensuration, capacity, etc.[6] As a result they have extended the use of the term proportionality to every similitude of relationships.[7] It is in this sense that we use the terms in the present study.

Division

25 Analogy of proportionality can occur in two ways—namely, metaphorically and properly.[8] It is *metaphorical*[9] when the common term

---

God and creature according to this mode." Cf. also in *I Sentent,* 19, 5, 2, *ad* 1 (quoted above in footnote 16 of Chapter One), *de Potentia* 7, 7, in *V Metaphysics* lect. 8, no. 879, *de Veritate,* 21, 4c and *ad* 3 quoted in footnote 14 of this chapter), etc.

2aCf. footnote 4 of Chapter Five.

3Cf. St. Thomas, *de Veritate* 23, 7, *ad* 9: "Proportion in the proper sense is found in quantities and means a definite measure of two quantities which are compared to one another . . . Nevertheless the name *proportion* has been widened to mean any relationship of one thing to another." Cf. also in *V Ethics,* lect. 5, no. 939 and *S. T.* I, 12, 1 *ad* 4.

4Cf. St. Thomas, e.g. in *V Ethics,* lect. 5, no. 940: "Proportionality is nothing but equality of proportion, i.e. the proportion of one to another is equal to the proportion of a third to a fourth."

5Cf. footnote 3.

6Cf. footnote 3, and also footnote 5 of Chapter One.

7Cf. footnote 2 of this chapter.

8Cf. St. Thomas, *de Veritate* 2, 11: [Analogy of proportionality] occurs in two ways. Sometimes the name implies in its primary meaning something in which no agreement can be found between God and creature, not even in the aforesaid manner [i.e. as sight with respect to eye and intellect]. This happens in all names which are symbolically predicated of God; e.g. when he is called a Lion, the Sun, or other names of the sort, for the definition of these has absolutely one formal meaning which is realized in one of the analogates and predicated of the other by metaphor.[10] For example, *to smile* has one meaning in itself, but is metaphorically analogous with respect to a true smile and a blooming meadow or good fortune; for thus we indicate that these things are just like a man smiling.[11] Sacred Scripture is full of examples of this sort of analogy wherever it teaches us about God by means of metaphors.

26 Analogy of proportionality occurs in the *proper* sense when the common name is predicated of both analogates[12] without the use of metaphors. For instance, *principle* can be predicated of the heart with respect to an animal and of a foundation with respect to a house. As Averroes says in his seventh commentary on *I Ethics,*[13] it is predicated of them proportionally.

---

things implies matter, which cannot be attributed to God. At other times, however, a name predicated of God and creature does not imply in its primary meaning anything in which the aforesaid mode of agreement cannot be found. This is the case with all things whose definition does not include any defect and which do not depend upon matter for their 'to be'; e.g. being, good, and such like things.

[9]Sometimes St. Thomas uses the expression "according to similitude" in the sense of "metaphorically"; e.g. *S. T.* I., 13, 9. Elsewhere, however, he makes clear that "a metaphor is not taken according to just any resemblance but according to an agreement in something which belongs to the proper nature of the thing whose name is transferred; e.g. the name *lion* is not transferred to God because of an agreement in sentient nature, but because of an agreement in some property of a lion," namely courage (*de Veritate* 7, 2). In *de Malo* 16, 1, *ad* 3 he makes clear that a metaphor refers to dynamic likeness. Cf. also *de Veritate* 2, 1; in *IV Sentent.* 45, 1, 1, *questiuncula* 1, *ad* 2; etc.

[10]Cf. Cajetan's commentary in *S. T.* I, 13, 3, (I): "To be predicated *in the proper sense* means that that what the name signifies is found in that of which it is predicated according to its own nature; to be predicated *metaphorically* means that what the name signifies is found in that of which it is predicated according to a likeness only."

[11]Cf. St. Thomas, *S. T. I,* 13, 6.

[12]In his commentary on *S. T.* I., 16, 6, (VI), Cajetan commenting upon the words: "When something is predicated analogously of many, it is found in only one of them according to its proper nature, and from this one the others are denominated," says: "This rule is not universal for every mode of analogy. On the contrary, as is clear from *I Ethics,* [ch. 6 (109 b 26ff)], properly speaking, it does not apply to any analogous name but only to names which are *to one, in one,* or *from one,* which, as we have said, are incorrectly called analogous."

[13]In *I Ethics,* ch. VI, ed. Venet, apud Juntas, 1550, vol. III, fol. 4, 21-39: "Hence they [things called good] do not have one and the same good in common in such a way that the name *good* is predicated of them univocally; likewise, it is not predicated of them in a purely equivocal sense so that they would have nothing in common except the name alone, for such things share nothing but their verbal expression. But it is more fitting to say that a name predicated of it [good things] belongs to one of the kinds of participation which is called *ambiguity,* and thus [*sic* instead of *si*] is as an *ambiguous* name [cf. no. 221]

Excellence

27 This analogy excells above the others mentioned above both by dignity and name. *By dignity,* because it arises from the genus of inherent formal causality,[14] for it predicates perfections that are inherent to each analogate, whereas the other analogy arises from extrinsic denomination.

28 It excells above the others *by name,* because only terms which are analogous by this type of analogy are called analogous by the Greeks, from whom we have borrowed the term. This, too, can be gathered from Aristotle, who in the *Metaphysics* refers to those names which we call analogous by attribution as *from one, to one* or *in one,* as is clear from Books IV and VII.[15] And when he defines unity by analogy in *V Metaphysics,*[16] he synonymously uses unity by analogy and unity by proportion[17] and defines as *one* in this way "whatever things are related to one another as one thing to another." Thus he clearly insinuates that the definition of analogates in the proper sense

---

which is predicated of many because they all [*omnia* instead of *omnino*] come from one intention, or because they tend to one end, or because they are predicated of many similar things; as e.g. the name *principle,* which is predicated of the heart in an animal and of the foundation in a wall, for the heart is related to the animal as the foundation is related to the wall. Likewise, the name *perfection* as predicated of the intellect and the senses, for the relation of the intellect to the soul is like the relation of the senses to the body. The more excellent of these three is that the name *good* is predicated of them in the way which is called according to proportionality."

[14]Cf. St. Thomas, *de Veritate,* 21, 4: "Everything is called good as *by an inherent form* by reason of its intrinsic similitude to the Highest Good, and further also by reason of the first goodness as the exemplary and efficient cause of all created goodness." And *de Veritate* 21, 4, *ad* 3: [Augustine's] words are to be understood in the sense that the divine goodness itself is declared to be the good of all good insofar as it is the first efficient and exemplary cause of all good, without exclusion, however, of the created goodness by which creatures are denominated good as *by an inherent form.*" And in *I Ethics,* lect. 7, no. 96: "[The Philosopher] prefers this third mode [i.e. according to proportionality] because it is taken according to goodness *inherent to* things."

[15]*Metaphysics* IV, 2, quoted in footnote 2 of Chapter Two; *Metaphysics* VII, 4 (1030a 34ff.): 'We apply the word *medical* by virtue of a *reference* to one and the same thing, nor yet speaking ambiguously; for a patient and an operation and an instrument are called medical neither by an ambiguity nor with a single meaning but with reference to a common end."

[16]Ch. 6 (1016b 32ff.): "Again, some things are one in number, others in species, other in genus, others by analogy; in number those whose matter is one, in species those whose definition is one, in genus those to which the same figure of predication applies, by analogy those which are related as a third thing is to a fourth."

[17]Aristotle's text does not have "by analogy or proportion," but St. Thomas in his commentary in *V Metaphysics,* lect. 8, no. 879, says: "One *by proportion or analogy* are those things which agree in this that one thing is to another as a third is to a fourth."

is the one we gave. The same idea, however, can be found more clearly in the Arabic translation which says: "Those things which are one by equality, i.e. by proportional equality, are those whose proportion is *one,* as the proportion of one thing to another." In his explanation of this text Averroes says: "Those things, too, are said to be *one* which are one by proportionality, just as for example the proportion of a governor to a city and of a helsman to a ship is one."[18] Moreover, in *II Posterior Analytics*[19] he calls such proportional names analogous.

What is more, in *I Ethics*[20] he distinguishes between the above mentioned terms *to one* or *from one* and analagous terms. Speaking of the community of *good* to those things which are said to be good, he says: "They are not considered similar to what is equivocal by chance, but certainly to 'being from one' or "all tending to one' or rather to what is one by analogy." Adding an example of analogy, he says, "Just as in the body there is sight, so in the soul there is intelligence."[21] In these words he not only reveals to a attentive reader that the name *analogy* expresses what we have said about it, but by using the word *rather* implies that this analogy must be preferred in metaphysical predications, as St. Thomas[22] excellently points out for the above mentioned reason.

Its Importance for Metaphysics

29 By means of analogy of proportionality we know indeed the intrinsic entity, goodness, truth, etc. of things, which are not known from the preceding analogy. For this reason, metaphysical speculations without knowledge of this analogy must be said to be unskilled. Those ignorant of this analogy suffer the same fate as those ancient philosophers who did not know logic, as is told in Book II of the *Sophistical Refutations.*[23] The situation has perhaps never been so

---

[18]*V Metaphysics.,* c. VI *"de uno,"* edit. Venet., apud Juntas, 1552, vol. VIII, fol. 54v, col. 1.

[19]*Posterior Analytics* II, 14 (98a 20ff.): "Yet a further method of selection is by analogy: for we cannot find a single identical name to give to a squid's pounce, a fish's spine, and an animal's bone, although these too possess common properties as if they were a single ossuous nature." St. Thomas, in *II Posterior Analytics,* lect. 17 (Leonine edition, no. 4) comments: "A further method of investigating in virtue of what character things possess a common attribute is to select what is common by *analogy, i.e. proportion."*

[20]Ch. 6; quoted in footnote 7 of Chapter One.

[21]*Nic. Ethics* I, 6 (1096b 29f.).

[22]In *I Ethics,* lect. 7, no. 96, quoted above in footnote 2 of this Chapter.

[23]Ch. 16 (175a 10ff.): "The man who is easily committed to a fallacy by some one else, and does not perceive it, is likely to incur this fate of himself

dangerous since the time of Aristotle as it is in our day—one is almost held guilty of blasphemy if one says that metaphysical terms are analogous and explains them as common by proportionality. Yet Averroes says in the above quoted text: "The more excellent of these three ways is that the name *good* be predicated of them in the way which is called according to proportionality."[24]

How Called by St. Thomas

30 This analogy is referred to by St. Thomas in *I Sentent.*[25] as analogy *"according to 'to be' and according to intention."* The reason is that the analogates are not considered equal in the perfection expressed by the common name, nor in the 'to be' of this perfection, yet they agree proportionally both in the perfection expressed by that name and in its 'to be.'

Since, as was mentioned, this question is obscure and very important, it will be necessary to explain it accurately and distinctly in several chapters.

---

also on many occasions." Cf. also Ch. 1 (165a 13ff.): "Just as in counting those who are not clever in manipulating their counters are taken in by the experts, in the same way in arguments, too, those who are not well acquainted with the force of names misreason both in their own discussions and when they listen to others."

[24]Cf. footnote 13 of this chapter.

[25]Cf. footnote 16 of Chapter One.

CHAPTER FOUR

THE DISTINCTION OF THE ANALOGON FROM THE ANALOGATES

Introduction

31 Since analogy is a mean between pure equivocation and univocation,[1] its nature should be explained by means of the extremes. And because names imply three elements, namely, the external word, the concept in the mind and the external thing or objective concept, we shall have to consider each one of these three and explain how the analogon is distinguished from the analogates.[2]

Distinction as Regards Things

32 *Definitions.* Let us start with the external things because they are prior to the concepts and the names. By an *equivocal* name diverse things are so signified that, as such, they are united only by the external word. By a *univocal* name diverse things are so signified that, as such, they are united into some thing which in itself is absolutely one, and which is abstracted and separated from them in the cognitive order. By an *analogous* name, however, diverse things are so signified that, as such, they are united to diverse things according to one proportion. It is to be noted that in the present question the word *thing* refers not only to a nature, but to any grade whatsoever, any reality whatsoever, and anything real which may be found in the external world.

33 *Difference Between the Foundation of Univocation and That of Analogy.* Hence the difference between univocation and analogy is the following. Things which give rise to *univocation* are similar to one another in the sense that the foundation of similitude in one has exactly the same nature as the foundation of similitude in the

[1]Cf. St. Thomas, *S. T.* I, 13, 5: "In this way some things are predicated of God and creatures analogously and not by pure equivocation nor by pure univocation . . . This mode of community is a mean between pure equivocation and simple univocation." Cf. in *IV Metaphysics,* lect. 1, no. 535 and in *XI Metaphysics,* lect. 3, no. 2197, etc.

[2]The term *analogon* is used as a translation of the Latin neuter *analogum* and may indicate the analogous term, the analogous notion, and the perfection or form in which the analogates, as such, agree.

other. Thus the notion of one contains in itself nothing which the notion of the other does not contain. In this way, the foundation of univocal similitude in both extremes abstracts equally from the extremes themselves. On the other hand, things which give rise to *analogy* are similar in the sense that the foundation of similitude in one is absolutely different in nature from the foundation of similitude in the other. Thus the notion of one thing does not contain in itself what the notion of the other contains. For this reason the foundation of analogous similitude in either of the extremes is not to be abstracted from the extremes themselves[3] but the foundations of similitude remain distinct, although they are similar according to proportion, and because of this they are said to be the same proportionally or analogically.

34 *Illustration of This Difference.* In order that the above explanations be clear to all they may be exemplified in the univocation of the term *animal* and the analogy of the term *being.* Man, ox, lion and other animals possess in themselves individual sensitive natures or their own animalities, which obviously are different in reality and similar to one another. Hence no matter in what extreme animality, which is the foundation of similitude, is considered absolutely, say, in a man or a lion, it will be found to abstract equally from its subject and not to include in one extreme anything which it does not include in the other.

Therefore, in virtue of their own animalities, man, ox, lion, etc. establish in the realm of reality a foundation of univocal similitude, which is called generic identity. In the cognitive order they are not unified into two or three animalities but in one only, which in the concrete is signified primarily and directly by the name *animal* and is indicated univocally by the common name *animal.* To all of them, insofar as they have a sensitive nature, the notion which is abstracted from all belongs without any distinctions whatsoever, and this notion is the adequate definition of what we have called *animality.*

---

[3]Cf. Le Rohellec, *op. cit.* p. 107: "In univocals perfect abstraction is made of the difference or dissimilitude; hence what the name signifies is wholly *one.* In analogy of proportionality the mind fastens its attention upon the common aspect and as much as possible tries to abstract from the differences. Since, however, the differences are essentially united to the common notion and inseparable from it, the intellect is not capable of prescinding perfectly from them. Although the common aspect is considered directly, nevertheless, no matter how much the differences are rendered obscure and relegated to the background, they always remain present and by their presence preclude the perfect unity of the concept and univocal predication."

On the other hand, substance, quantity, quality, etc. do not have in their quiddities anything which can be abstracted in the way just mentioned, say, entity, for there is nothing else above substantiality; consequently there cannot be any substantial univocation between
35 them. Despite the fact that their quiddities are not only diverse but even primarily diverse, they do retain a similitude in this that each of them has a 'to be' proportioned to itself.

Hence in the order of reality, on the one hand, they give rise to an analogous, i.e. proportional, similitude, not because of some quiddity of the same nature in the extremes, but because of their own quiddities insofar as these quiddities are proportioned to their own 'to be-s.' In the intellect, on the other hand, they are united to as many things as there are foundations. These things are unified by a similitude of proportion, and because of this similitude they are indicated by the term *being* and analogically referred to by the common name *being*. Thus it is clear that it is in a different manner that things are unified under an analogous and a univocal name.

Distinction as Regards Concepts

36 *In Univocation There Is One Concept.* The mental concept, also, is not found in the same way in univocal and analogous names. The univocal name and all the univocates, as such, have in the mind only one concept which corresponds to them perfectly and adequately. For the foundation of univocal similitude, which is what is formally signified by the univocal term, is of absolutely the same nature in all the univocates; hence in the representation of one, of necessity all are represented.

In Analogy There Is a Double Concept. In analogous names, on the other hand, the foundations of analogous similitude are of a different nature absolutely, and of the same nature to a certain extent, i.e. by proportion. Hence we must distinguish a twofold mental concept of the analogous name—one perfect and the other imperfect—and we must say that to the analogous name and its analogates there corresponds one *imperfect* mental concept, and as many *perfect* concepts as there are analogates.[4] For one analogate, as such, being similar to the other, it follows that the concept representing one analogate represents also the other, in virtue of the maxim: What

[4]Cf. in the appendix Cajetan's *The Concept of Being,* nos. 3 ff., where he answers the objections of Sylvester of Ferrara.

ever bears a likeness to something similar, as such, is similar also to a third which is similar to the second.[5]

37 *In What Sense There Is a Double Concept in Analogy.* Since the similitude referred to is only according to a proportion, which is of a different nature in the other foundation, the concept perfectly representing one analogate falls short of giving a perfect representation of the other; consequently there must be another adequate concept of the other analogate. Hence the assertions that the analogon has one mental concept and that it has several are both true in different ways. Nevertheless, absolutely speaking, it would be better to say that the analogon has several concepts,[6] unless the scope of the discussion

---

[5]Cf. below, no. 106 and *The Concept of Being,* no. 3.

[6]Cf. his commentary in *de Ente et Essentia,* Ch. I (Laurent ed. q. 2, no. 14), quoted in footnote 2 of the Appendix.

Sylvester of Ferrara, however, in his commentary in *I Contra Gentes,* Ch. 34 (Leonine ed. XII-XV) disagrees: "As regards this difficulty [whether *being* has one concept or not], there are various opinions among Thomists. Some . . . hold that *being* and also other names which are predicated of God and creatures by analogy express one formal or mental concept which prescinds from the concepts of the other things, although it does not express an objective concept which is one by precision, but a concept which is one by analogy. Others hold that *being* neither expresses one adequate mental concept which prescinds from the concepts of its inferiors nor an objective concept, but say that, just as it expresses the analogates in so far as proportionally one or similar, so also it expresses the mental concepts of the analogates in so far as they are one concept proportionally.

(XIII) The second of these opinions seems more truthful to me and more in conformity with the teachings of the philosophers and St. Thomas. To understand this assertion one should take into consideration that, since being is predicated essentially and quidditatively of things, we may speak of its concept in two ways. In one way, we may speak about the concept of what the thing is, in which sense [being] is predicated adequately and quidditatively of all the analogates. In another sense, we may speak about the imperfect and inadequate concept of what the name expresses. I call the concept perfect and adequate, not only by adequacy of predication, but also by adequacy of representation, because it is not only predicated of all beings, but also perfectly represents the nature of the thing signified primarily and directly by the name *being.*

If there is question of the first concept, I say that *being* has neither one mental concept nor one objective concept which prescinds from the others. My first reason is that it would be impossible to avoid making being univocal . . .

(XIV) My second reason is that St. Thomas . . . says that substance is put into the definition of accident in so far as being . . . Therefore, the concept of being is not one by precision from the concepts of substance and accident . . . Moreover, . . . when St. Thomas speaks professionally about this matter, he says that according to the same notion nothing can belong to God and creatures [*S. T.* I, 13, 5; *de Potentia* 7, 7; *de Veritate* 2, 11; etc.].

(XV) If, however, there is question of the imperfect and inadequate concept pertaining to what the name expresses (*quid nominis*), there is no difficulty in admitting that being expresses one concept which prescinds from the others . . . Hence we must say that being does not have one perfect and adequate

requires a different answer. I say this—in a discussion with those who say that analogous characters do not at all have one mental concept, one should not reply that their concept expresses something absolutely unified.[7]

Accordingly, the reader should use great discretion whenever he finds it written in one place that the analogates agree in one notion and then finds it said in another that they do not agree in one notion.[8]

38 *Difference Between the Mental Concepts of Analogous and Univocal Perfections.* Thus the difference between analogy and univocation with respect to the mental concept is as follows. The *univocal* and its univocates, as such, have one concept which corresponds to them perfectly and adequately, as is clear from the concept of *animal.*

On the other hand, the *analogon* and its analogates, as such, of necessity have several concepts which represent them perfectly and one concept which represents them imperfectly. This assertion, however, should not be understood as if there is one concept adequately corresponding to the analogous name and inadequately to the analogates, for such a name would really be univocal. The sense is that one concept which perfectly represents one of two analogates, as such, imperfectly represents the other.

With respect to the external word, however, there is no difference between analogous and univocal characters.

Distinction of the Analogon From the Analogates

39 After these preliminary considerations, it is easy to solve the problem proposed in this chapter, viz. how an analogon say, *being,*

---

mental concept which prescinds [from its inferiors], but immediately expresses the concepts of substance, quantity, quality and the others, in so far as they are one by similitude or proportion."

[7]The Latin has: *dico autem hoc: quoniam cum secundum dicentes* (first Venet. ed.; *cum contradicentes,* Parisian ed.; *cum contradicendus,* Lyons ed. and Venetian ed. 1588), *analoga omnino carere uno conceptu mentali, sermo est; unum eorum conceptum absolute dicere non est reprehendendum."* The very multiplicity of readings shows the obscurity of this sentence. The above translation is the best we can make of it.

[8]Cf. Cajetan's commentary in *de Ente et Essentia, cap.* II (q. 3, no. 21, in Laurent edition): "The analogous is a mean between the purely equivocal and the univocal, just as between absolutely the same and absolutely diverse the mean is "the same to a certain extent and diverse to a certain extent." As a mean it resembles the nature of both extremes, for it expresses in some way several notions and in some way one notion. For this reason one may find sometimes in outstanding philosophers that the analogon expresses several notions and at other times that it expresses one notion."

is distinguished from its analogates, say, substance, quantity and quality.[9]

Distinction as Regards the Objective Concept. A *univocal,* say, *animal,* is distinguished from its univocates, such as man and lion, both as regards the thing signified or the objective concept and as regards the mental concept just as what is absolutely one by abstraction etc. is distinguished from what is absolutely many etc.

An *analogon,* however, with respect to the thing or the objective concept, is distinguished [from the analogates] just as what is one by proportion from what is many absolutely, or what amounts to the same, just as many insofar as they are similar according to proportions are distinguished from what is many absolutely. For example, *being* is not distinguished from substance and quantity because it signifies something common to them, but because substance implies only the quiddity of substance, and likewise quantity simply signifies the quiddity of quantity; whereas *being* signifies both quiddities insofar as they are similar according to their proportions to their 'to be-s.' That is, it expresses them insofar as they are proportionally the same.

40 *Distinction as Regards the Mental Concept.* With respect to the *adequate* mental concept, the distinction has to be made in exactly the same way.

As regards the *imperfect* mental concept, although it is distinguished [from the analogates] just as what is one absolutely from what is many absolutely, nevertheless it is not distinguished from them as the one which abstracts from the many in representation, as is the case with univocal terms. For from the foregoing it is clear that that concept, say, of quality insofar as it is a being, is an adequate representation of one of the analogates, viz. of quality itself, insofar as concerns its relationship to its own 'to be' and does not abstract from the quiddity of quality. Of the other analogates, however, such as quantity and substance, the concept is an imperfect representation insofar as it is similar to them proportionally.

---

[9]Cf. Cajetan's commentary in *S. T.* I, 13, 5, X: "An analogous concept is different from its inferiors, but not in the way a univocal concept differs from its univocates. The univocal concept differs [from its inferiors] in so far as it is prescinded from them, whereas the analogous concept differs in so far as it contains them."

CHAPTER FIVE

ABSTRACTION OF THE ANALOGON FROM THE ANALOGATES

Two Difficulties

41 Upon the basis of the foregoing considerations we must now show how the analogon abstracts from those things to which it is said to be common by analogy; e.g. how *being* abstracts from substance and quantity. For there is a certain difficulty in this matter, not only on the part of the things, but also on the part of the concept.

First Difficulty. On the part of the *things* a difficulty arises because it seems that the thing signified by the analogous name is abstractible and abstracted in the same way as a thing signified by a univocal name. As we read in *V Metaphysics,*[1] "unity in quality makes similar." Hence there appears to be no reason why it should be possible to abstract a unified thing[1a] from certain similar objects but not from others, although it is evident why from some similar things, such as Socrates[2] and Plato, a more unified thing can be abstracted, and from others, such as man and stone, only a less unified one. Hence if substance and quantity are similar in that they both are *being,* and thus there is in them some one thing which is the foundation of this similitude, what is to prevent our abstracting from them this one thing that is common to both?

42 *Second Difficulty.* On the part of the *concept* a difficulty arises because the concept of an analogon seems to abstract from the analogates in the same way as the univocal abstracts from the univocates. For the analogous name confusedly implies the individual proportions of the analogates and distinctly signifies only the proportion in common.

For example, *being* does not mean something having a reference to 'to be' in this or that particular way, say, as a substance or as quantity. If being is a proportional name, it seems to signify some-

[1]Ch. 9 (1018a 15f.): "Those things are called 'like' which have the same attributes in every respect, and those which have more attributes the same than different, and those whose quality is one." St. Thomas' commentary in *V Metaphysics,* lect. 12, no. 918, has: "Unity in quality makes similar."

[1a]Concerning the meaning of *thing,* see above, no. 32.

[2]Cf. footnote 12 of Chapter Three.

thing having a reference to 'to be' according to some proportion, whatever this proportion may be. Such a thing, however, clearly is equally abstracted from substance and from quantity. Consequently, in analogous terms the abstraction of the concept appears to take place in the same way as in univocals.

How the Analogon Abstracts From the Analogates

43 *Preliminary Notions.* In order that the solution of this ambiguity become clear it should be kept in mind that *to abstract* does not mean the same when we say that the intellect abstracts *animal* from *man* and *horse* and when we say that *animal* abstracts from *man* and *horse.* In the first case, to abstract means the very operation of the intellect apprehending in them one thing and not the others. In the second case, it means an extrinsic denomination, derived from this operation of the intellect, by which the thing known is called *abstracted.* Nevertheless, abstraction always amounts to one and the same thing because it always means that one thing is apprehended by the intellect while the other is not.

44 Therefore, to consider the abstraction of the analogon from the analogates is nothing else than to investigate and determine how the thing signified by the analogous name can be understood without the analogates being understood at the same time, and how the concept of the analogon may be had without the concepts of the analogates.

45 *Abstraction of the Analogon From the Analogates.* From the foregoing considerations and from the very word *analogy* itself,[3] it is clear that an analogous name does not signify something which is absolutely one but something which is one by proportion, and that what is one by proportion is the same as diverse things insofar as they are proportionally similar.[4] Hence we can readily conclude that an analogous perfection can be understood without the analogates being understood at the same time, and consequently that it abstracts from them.

46 This assertion, however, is not to be taken in the sense in which the one thing is understood in univocal terms, as for example, sensitive

[3]Cf. footnotes 5 and 8 of Chapter One, and no. 23.

[4]As Le Rohellec remarks, in analogy of proportionality "it does not matter whether one says *the same* or *similar* because in the present question these terms are in perfect agreement. Once numerical identity is excluded, there remains only formal identity, i.e. identity according to univocal or analogous similitude." *Op. cit.,* p. 106, footnote 18.

nature or animal is understood without any understanding of human or equine nature taken as such. It should be taken in the sense in which two things are understood as proportionately similar without these two things being understood at the same time with respect to their proper natures taken absolutely. Thus the abstraction of the analogon does not consist in the cognition of one thing and the non-cognition of the other, but in the understanding of one and the same thing as such and its non-understanding in an absolute sense. For example, the abstraction of *being* does not consist in this that beingness is apprehended while substance or quantity are not, but in this that substance or quantity is apprehended as having a certain relationship to its own 'to be' (for it is in this that proportional similitude is found), while substance or quantity is not apprehended absolutely. The same applies to all other analogous things, as are almost all metaphysical things.[4a]

47 Accordingly, it can be admitted that something analogous in one way abstracts and in another way does not abstract from the analogates. Insofar as it abstracts from them, it abstracts from them just as the analogon as such, i.e. as something similar to another proportionally, abstracts from itself considered absolutely. It does not abstract from them insofar as the analogon taken as such necessarily includes itself and cannot be understood without itself. The same cannot be said of univocals because something univocal can be apprehended without the others to which it is univocally common, in such a way that the univocal in no way includes in its concept the subjects to which it is common, as is clear in *animal*.

Solution of the First Difficulty

48 The objection[5] to the contrary which was taken from the nature of analogous similitude is easily answered. Since unity is spoken of in various ways, every similitude does not have to be according to absolute unity.[6] Sometimes it is sufficient that simiItude arises

---

[4a]For instance, being and its transcendentals, thing, something, one, true, good, beautiful; act and potency; substance and accident; cause in general, efficient and final cause with respect to their inferiors; perfection, life, intellect, will, action; truth, cognition, vision, judgment, analogy, etc.

[5]Cf. no. 41.

[6]Cf. St. Thomas, *S. T.* I, 4, 3: "Since similitude is based upon agreement or communication in form, it is multiplied according to the many modes in which there can be communication in a form. Some things are called similar because they communicate in the same form *according to the same mode (rationem) and according to the same measure;* and these things are

through proportional unity. Now what is one proportionally is not absolutely one, but many which are similar by proportion. Hence it is impossible to abstract from these many something which is absolutely one, for the very similitude itself is only proportional, and its foundation is only proportionally one.

49 It is of the very nature of proportional unity to have four terms, as is said in *V Ethics.*[7] For the proportionality from which the similitude of proportions arises must have at least four terms, which are the extremes of the two proportions. Consequently, what is one by proportion is not unified absolutely, but, retaining its distinction, it is one and said to be one only insofar as it is not divided by dissimilar proportions. Hence just as there is no other reason why proportional unity is not absolute unity except that this is its formal nature, so too we must not look for another reason why from proportionally similar things [an absolutely] one thing cannot be abstracted —the only reason is that proportional similitude in its very nature includes such a diversity. Those who want to proceed further in this matter happen to be looking for something that cannot be the object of a question, as for example, why man is a rational animal, etc.

Solution of the Second Difficulty

50 The same must be said with respect to the abstraction of the concept. The concept of an analogous name does not abstract from what is absolutely many as something which is absolutely one, but as something which is proportionally one, i.e. as what is similar according to proportions.

---

said to be not merely similar but equal in their similitude, as two equally white things are said to be similar in whiteness, and this is the most perfect similitude. In another way, things are called similar because they communicate in a form *according to the same mode (rationem), though not according to the same measure,* but according to more or less, as something less white is said to be similar to something more white; and this is imperfect similitude. In a third way, things are called similar because they communicate in the same form, but *not according to the same mode* (*rationem*), as is seen in non-univocal agents . . . In this way, whatever things come from God, insofar as they are beings, are similar to Him as the first and universal principle of all being." Concerning the translation of *ratio* by *mode,* see Le Rohellec, *op. cit.,* p. 109: In this text *"ratio* is distinguished against form or perfection and therefore expresses the mode of having the form. In this sense *ratio* signifies nothing but diversity." Cf. also *de Potentia 7, 7 ad* 3, and Cajetan's commentary in *S. T.* I, 4, 3, (II).

[7]Ch. 3 (1131a 32ff.): "Proportion is equality of ratios and involves four terms at least (that discrete proportion involves four terms is plain, but so does continuous proportion, for it uses one term as two and mentions it twice)." Cf. St. Thomas, in *V Ethics,* lect. 5, no. 940.

51 However, in the second objection[8] there was question of the abstraction of an analogous concept from the special concepts of that analogy, and the analogates were incorrectly called there partial notions of the analogon. Hence great care must be taken lest the appearance spoken of in the objection lead to the error mentioned in it.

Abstraction of the Analogous Concept in Analogy of Attribution. In analogy of attribution all the analogates agree in that they refer to exactly the same form in such a way that they agree not only in one term, but also in having a reference to it. Nevertheless it should be kept in mind that in analogy of attribution it is wrong to attribute to the analogon a unified concept of a common reference to this term by means of abstraction from this and that particular reference.

Let us explain the matter by an example. Animal as healthy, urine as healthy, medicine as healthy, agree in having health as their term, animal being its subject, urine its sign, and medicine its cause. They agree also in having a reference to health, for each of them has a relation to health, although in a different way. Nevertheless from these special relationships there is not abstracted a common reference to health, expressed by the name *healthy,* in whose concept the special relationships to health are included confusedly and potentially.

52 For it is not true that healthy signifies what I call "pertaining or related in some way to health."

First of all, because if this were the case, the name *healthy* would really be univocal with respect to urine, animal, etc., as is evident from the definition of univocal terms.

Secondly, because it is against the intention of those who call urine or a diet healthy. If any one inquires what urine is insofar as it is healthy, the answer is not "something having a relation to health," but everyone specifies this relationship and says "a sign of health." Likewise, the answer with respect to a diet is that it is preservative of health, etc.

Thirdly, because it is contrary to all philosophers and logicians, at least those whom I have consulted thus far.

53 *Abstraction of the Analogous Concept in Analogy of Proportionality.* Just as in cases of analogy of attribution we must beware of the above-mentioned error, so with respect to what is analogous by pro-

---

[8]Cf. no. 42.

portion, which alone, absolutely speaking, is analogous, we must be on our guard against a similar error, which for a similar reason has the appearance of soundness.

Because the analogates agree in that each of them is something commensurate or proportionate, although in a different way, one could get the impression that from these special proportions a common proportionate [quiddity] is abstracted and signified by the analogous name. In this way the analogon would have one concept in which all the special proportions of the analogates would be included confusedly and potentially.

Let us explain it by an example. Substance is proportioned to its own 'to be,' and likewise quantity and quality, although in a different way. Therefore, from substance, quantity, quality, etc., which are differently proportioned to their 'to be-s', there would be abstracted a thing or quiddity having a proportion to 'to be,' whatever might be this proportion. This, then would be what is primarily signified by *being,* and in this all the individual proportions of substance, quality, quantity, etc. to their own 'to be-s' would be included confusedly and potentially.

54 However, this idea is absolutely false. First of all, because what is predicated, namely, "something which is proportioned to 'to be,' " is not absolutely one thing in objective reality except in the imagination.

Secondly, because the proportional names would be univocal, as is clear from the definition of univocals. Consequently, the result would be the destruction of the notion of proportionality, which does not allow the extremes to be absolutely one; hence these extremes would be proportional and not proportional, which the intellect in no way can admit.

Thirdly, because it is explicitly against the authority of Aristotle in *II Posterior Analytics,*[9] which will be quoted later,[10] and in *I Ethics,*[11] which has been quoted above, against the Saintly Doctor,[12] and against both Averroes[13] and Albert.[14]

---

[9]Ch. 14; quoted in footnote 19 of Chapter Three.
[10]No. 109.
[11]Ch. 6; quoted in footnote 7 of Chapter One.
[12]In *I Ethics,* lect. 7, no. 96; quoted in footnote 2 of Chapter Three.
[13]In *I Ethics,* Ch. VI; quoted in footnote 2 of Chapter Three.
[14]In *I Ethics, tract.* II, *c.* 4: "As has been mentioned, when a comparison is made of good things, this comparison must be made in some one nature

Hence the confusion by which an analogon, whether according to attribution or according to proportion, implies the special relations or proportions is not a confusion of several concepts into one common concept, but a confusion of significations into one word. This confusion does not take place in a uniform way. In analogy of attribution, the analogous term signifies the primary analogate distinctly and the others confusedly. In analogy of proportion, the analogous term is permitted to be related indistinctly to all its significations.

Additional Explanations About the Abstraction of the Analogon

55 Prudence and careful attention is necessary in this matter. For the notions of an analogon may be taken in two ways, namely, either in themselves or insofar as they are the same. Insofar as they are the same because of the nature of proportional identity, they do not abstract from themselves. Nevertheless, by reason of their identity, or insofar as they are the same, there pertains to them something which does not pertain to them by reason of their diversity, as is clear from what is common to them. Hence two apparently irreconcilable characteristics are seen to belong to the notions of the analogon—namely, on the one hand, that these notions insofar as they are the same do not abstract from themselves, and on the other, that these notions insofar as they are the same cause and have something which they do not have insofar as they are diverse. Thus they can be reduplicated insofar as they are the same without being reduplicated insofar as they are diverse.

Proportional identity claims for itself these two characteristics not only as compatible but as necessary. For, on the one hand, while it does not allow the extremes to be wholly unified it does not allow itself to be wholly abstracted from them; but on the other hand, while positing the extremes as in some way undivided and the same, it requires that it must be possible for them to be considered and reduplicated as the same.

56 Thus it happens that when the identity contained in an analogon is compared to the difference of notions also included in it, a certain

---

which is present in the things compared. This nature, however, does not have to be generic or specific, but rather something which belongs to all according to proportion. In such things the nature in which the comparison is made is in one primarily and directly according to its essence, and in the others through a respect to this one thing. Hence pure goodness is the highest good, which is God or the idea of good, as Plato says. The others are good because they are imitations or echoes of this good."

abstraction is found, which is not so much abstraction as a mode of abstraction. Because of this abstraction an analogon, say, *being,* is said to abstract not only from its analogates, such as substance and quantity, as we mentioned above,[15] but from the very notions contained in it, i.e. from the diversity of the very notions contained in it; for instance, from the notion of being as it is in substance and from the notion of being as it is in quantity.

The reason is not that the analogon expresses some notion common to them, because this is foolish; nor that these notions are exactly the same or that it unifies them absolutely, for in this case it would not be analogous but univocal. The reason is that it unifies them proportionally, signifies them as the same proportionally, and thus presents them to be considered as the same. Concealing, as it were, the inseparably concomitant diversity, it both unites the diversity of notions by proportional identity and confuses them in a certain way.

57 Thus to the analogon is proper not only the confusion of meanings in the external word, but there is also a confusion of concepts or notions in their proportional identity, yet in such a way that not so much the concepts as the diversity of these concepts is confused.

It is because the analogon principally implies such an identity, and because we make frequent use of such a confusion and say that analogous names abstract from every diversity of its notions when we explain that it repeatedly stands confusedly for all, that not a little care is necessary lest we fall into univocation.

Summary

58 Thus the analogon abstracts from its analogates, for instance, *being* from substance and quantity, as what is one by proportion abstracts from many, or as things which are proportionally similar abstract from themselves taken absolutely, both as regards the objective and the mental concept, whether there be question of total or formal abstraction. For with respect to the same thing these two abstractions do not differ except according to precision and non-precision, as we have explained elsewhere.[16] Hence to say that *being* is

---

[15]Cf. above, no. 46.

[16]In *de Ente et Essentia, prooemium* (Laurent ed. q. I, no. 51): "Just as there is a twofold composition, viz. of form with matter and of a whole with its parts, so also is there a twofold abstraction by the intellect—namely, one by which the formal is abstracted from the material, and one by which a universal whole is abstracted from its subjective parts. In the first way *quantity* is abstracted from sensible matter, and in the second way *animal*

abstracted from the natures of the predicaments by formal abstraction is nothing else than saying that predicamental natures are proportioned to their own 'to be-s' taken precisely as such. From the special

---

is abstracted from ox and lion. I call the first abstraction *formal* because what is abstracted by this type of abstraction is as a form of that of which it is abstracted. The second abstraction I call *total* because what is abstracted by it is as a universal whole with respect to that from which it is abstracted.

These two abstractions differ in four ways. *First,* because in *formal* abstraction the two concepts are complete separately, viz. the concept of that which is abstracted, and the concept of that from which abstraction is made, i.e. the formal and the material concept, so that one concept does not include the other. For instance, a line insofar as a line has a complete definition which does not include sensible matter; and conversely the sensible matter of a line has a complete definition which does not include anything of the line insofar as a line, for otherwise the definition of natural things would abstract from sensible matter. In *total* abstraction, however, the two concepts do not remain complete separately in such a way that the one does not include the other, but only one [of them does not include the other], namely [the concept] of that which is abstracted. For example, when I abstract *animal* from man, the concepts of man and ox do not prescind from one another, but only the concept of animal does not include the concept of man, for man is not intelligible without animal. The foundation of this difference is that this abstraction comes about through the consideration of something having the nature of an inferior and the removal or non-consideration of something [else] having the nature of the same inferior; for *animal* is abstracted from man by this that the intellect considers in man "animal" and not "rational," both of which belong to the nature of man. The first abstraction, however, does not come about through the consideration of something having the nature of matter and the non-consideration* of something [else] that is [also] of this nature, but rather by the separation of what belongs to the formal nature from what belongs to the material nature, and vice versa, as is clear from the example given.

Secondly, by means of formal abstraction, actuality, distinction and intelligibility arise in that which is abstracted, whereas in total abstraction confusion of potentiality and less intelligibility arise in that which is abstracted.

Thirdly, in formal abstraction the more a thing is abstracted, the better known its nature, whereas in total abstraction the more a thing is abstracted the less it is known to us.**

The foundation of these differences is that formal abstraction is made by means of separation from potential matters and the like, whereas total abstraction is made by means of separation from specific actualities, and the more a thing is abstracted from them, the more potential it is (for a genus potentially contains its inferiors) and the less intelligible (for act as such is better known than potency. Cf. *VI Metaphysics,* [1(1025b 28ff.); St. Thomas, lect. 1, no. 1144ff.]). *Fourthly,* they differ because diversity of measure of formal abstraction specifies speculative sciences, as is clear from *VI Metaphysics* [Ch. 1 (1025b 1ff.), St. Thomas, lect. 1, no. 1145]. Total abstraction, however, is common to all science and for this reason the metaphysical as such is not compared to the physical as the universal whole to subjective parts, but as the formal to the material, as is the case also with the mathematical. For, although metaphysical grades are more universal than others and can be compared to others as to their subjective parts because both types of abstraction can be used with respect to the same thing, nevertheless, insofar as they are objects of metaphysical consideration, they are not universals with respect to the physical, but forms, of which natural things are the matter as should be duly noted.

or individual notions in the extremes of the analogy it abstracts in a way, not by a third simple concept, but by the common name and the proportional identity of these notions.

Thus it is clear how *being* sometimes has formal abstraction, namely, when it is taken in precision from the other genera and specific notions, and how sometimes it has total abstraction, namely, when it is considered as a universal whole which potentially includes the other genera and species.

---

*Reading *per non considerationem* instead of *non per considerationem.*

***Tanto notius* obviously is a mistake and should be *tanto minus notum.*

CHAPTER SIX

PREDICATION OF THE ANALOGON OF ITS ANALOGATES

Two Difficulties

59 *First Difficulty.* From the foregoing perhaps someone will get the impression that the predication of an analogon of its analogates, e.g. *being* of substance and quantity, or *form* of soul and whiteness, etc., is like the predication of the equivocal of its equivocates. Thus analogous predication would not be the predication of the superior of its inferiors, nor of the more common of the less common, except in a purely verbal sense, but the predication of a thing of itself. For an analogon does not signify one thing which is realized in both analogates; without such a realization, however, it is not possible to have predication of the superior or more common by intrinsic denomination or inherence. Yet it is in this way that what is analogous by proportionality was declared to be common.

60 *Second Difficulty.* An argument based upon *I Topics*[1] can also be used in strong support of this opinion. It is as follows. Apart from being verbally common, an analogon is either a convertible or an inconvertible predicate. Now it is clear that it is not inconvertible, for substance insofar as it is related in this way to its 'to be'—which is what *being* means when predicated of substance—is convertible with substance; likewise quantity insofar as it is commensurate in that way to its 'to be' is convertible with quantity; and the same goes for other examples. Hence it follows that an analogon cannot be predicated of its analogates as something superior. For what has been proved to be convertible cannot assume the role of something superior.

The Analogon Is Predicated of the Analogates as the Superior of its Inferiors

61 *Proof.* An analogon is truly predicated of its analogates as something superior and is common to them, not only with respect to the external

[1]Ch. 8 (103b 8ff.): "For every predicate of a subject must of necessity be either convertible with its subject or not: and if it is convertible, it would be its definition or property, for if it signifies the essence, it is the definition; if not, it is a property."

word, but also with respect to one and the same concept proportionally. The unity of such a concept is sufficient to make the predicate have the character of something superior, for *superior* means nothing else than that one predicate extends to several things. Now it is clear that what is one by proportion is not one by accident nor by aggregation, as a pile of rocks, but in itself. For a clear understanding of this truth one should start with a consideration of the extremes[2] and keep in mind that the analogon is midway between the univocal and the equivocal; hence it follows that an analogon predicates of its analogates in one way the same thing, and in another way not the same thing.

As is evident from the preceding chapter,[3] an analogon predicates something which abstracts in a certain way from the analogates. Hence it follows that it is compared to its analogates as the greater to the lesser or as the superior to the inferior, although what it predicates of them is not absolutely one in nature.

62 *Illustration of This Proof.* In order that this proof may become clearer it can be exemplified in the following way. In univocal as well as in equivocal and analogous terms the following foursome is found—at least, two equivocates, univocates or analogates, and two things or natures of things which give rise to equivocation, univocation, or analogy. For example, in the equivocation of *dog* this foursome is found—the dogfish,[4] the ordinary dog, the nature of the former, and the nature of the latter as indicated by the term *dog.* In the univocation of *animal* there is also a foursome—man, ox, the sensitive nature of man and that of the ox, which give rise to the univocation of *animal.* In the analogy of *being,* likewise, there is a foursome—substance, quantity, substance as commensurate to its 'to be,' and quantity as proportioned to its 'to be.'

63 The first two, namely, the equivocates and the analogates, are distinguished in all these in the same way insofar as our problem is concerned, for in all cases they are co-distinguished from their opposite. The other two, however, which serve as the foundation of univocation, equivocation and analogy, are unified or distinguished in different ways.

As regards *equivocals,* those natures—that of the dogfish and that of the ordinary dog—are entirely different in nature. For this reason

---

[2]i.e. univocation and equivocation.
[3]Cf. no. 46.
[4]*Canis marinus.*

whatever *dog* predicates of a dogfish it in no way predicates of an ordinary dog, and vice versa. Therefore, it is only with respect to the name that an equivocal term is said to be, and really is, more common or greater than the equivocates.

64 As regards *univocals,* those natures—animality in an ox and animality in a lion—although diverse in number and species, nevertheless are exactly the same in nature. For the nature of one is exactly the same as that of the other, and vice versa. For this reason exactly the same thing which *animal* predicates of man it predicates also of an ox. Therefore it is said to be univocal and superior to man, lion and ox.

65 As regards *analogous* terms, however, the things which are the foundation of the analogy—say, *quantity* insofar as it is related in this way to its 'to be' and *substance* insofar as it is related in that way to its 'to be'—are diverse in number, species and genus; nevertheless they are the same in nature, not absolutely but proportionally, for the notion of one is proportionally the same as that of the other.

66 For this reason, the very same thing which the analogous term predicates, say, what *being* predicates of quantity, it also predicates proportionally of substance, and vice versa. For it is proportionally the selfsame thing which it posits in substance, and vice versa. Hence an analogon like *being* is more common, greater or superior to the analogates not only in a purely verbal sense but in its concept, which, as was said, is proportionally one.

Accordingly, an analogon and a univocal are similar in this that both have the character of something more common or superior. They differ, however, insofar as the analogon is superior analogically or proportionally, and the univocal univocally.

The Identity of Nature in Univocation and Analogy

67 [The correctness of this conclusion is] justly [asserted], for the foundation of superiority is found in both, but not that of univocation. Superiority is based upon the notional identity of the thing signified, i.e. upon the fact that the thing signified is not found in this one analogate only, but the selfsame thing is found also in the other, not numerically but according to notion. Univocation, on the other hand, is based upon the mode of absolute identity. I mean [absolute] notional

identity of the thing signified, i.e. upon this that the notion of the thing signified is exactly the same in this thing and in that thing.

68 Although in analogous terms we do not find this mode of identity, which we have so often said is found in univocals, nevertheless identity itself of notions is found in them. For proportional identity is a kind of identity. Therefore, an analogon, such as *being,* is no less a superior predicate than a univocal, such as *animal,* although in a different way. For an analogon is superior proportionally because it is founded on the proportional notional identity of the thing signified; whereas a univocal [is superior] by precision and absolutely because its superiority is based upon the absolute notional identity of the thing signified. For this reason St. Thomas in considering the foundation of superiority says in *V Metaphysics*[5] that *being* is superior to all, as *animal* is superior to man and ox.

Solution of the First Difficulty

69 From the foregoing it follows that the objections brought forward against our thesis err in that they do not make a distinction between identity and mode of identity. We grant that in order that a term may be called superior or more common it must posit one and the same thing in both [inferiors]. However, the fallacy of the consequent is committed if from this one draws the conclusion that the term must predicate exactly one and the same thing [of both inferiors]. All the time there is question of identity in notion or definition. But identity and unity include not only absolute unity and identity, but also proportional identity, which is found in the notion of an analogous name. Therefore, it must be denied that in analogous terms the same thing is not predicated of one and the other analogate, for proportionally, one and the same thing is predicated of all the analogates; consequently, [this predicate] must be placed among those predicates which are not convertible. For example, although quantity equals being as realized in quantity according to exactly the same notion, it does not equal it according to this notion taken proportionally, for the selfsame notion of being proportionally extends itself to substance and quantity. Still, since it is proportional identity which is expressed by the analogon, it cannot at all be conceded that by corresponding formally to such concepts the analogon can be converted with any particular analogate.

---

[5]Lect. 9, no. 896: "For being is superior to each and every being, just as animal is to man."

Solution of the Second Difficulty

70 However, let us get down to the analogates themselves.[6] Because an analogon predicates a notion which is one only by proportion, and because what is proportionally one is the same as many that are similar according to proportions, it can be said without fear that the analogon may be compared to the analogates in two ways. In one way, *absolutely,* and in this way the analogon can be converted with each of the analogates according to the particular notion of each because no notion of the analogon is found to be exactly the same in two analogates. In another way, *according to the proportional identity* which one notion has with the other, and in this way the analogon cannot be converted with any analogate because the notions of the analogon are proportionately undivided, and one notion is the other proportionally.

Since, as was said, an analogon expresses this type of identity, therefore, formally and absolutely speaking, it must be admitted that the analogon is an inconvertible and more common predicate. Nevertheless it is not a genus, species, property, definition, difference or accident in the manner of a universal.

On this account no discredit is thrown upon the prestige of Aristotle[7] or of Porphyry[8] because they were concerned with the exploration of the predicables, which are absolutely one, and consequently placed analogous terms among the equivocals.

Concluding Remarks

71 From the foregoing it is manifestly evident that an analogon does not imply and predicate a disjunct concept, nor a concept which is one by precision and unequally participated in, nor a concept which is one by order, but a concept which is one by proportion.[9] However, as regards the order included in analogous terms, we shall have to see about it later.[10] Therefore, when *being* is predicated of man or whiteness or anything else, the sense is not that it is a substance or an accident, but that it is something related in such a way to 'to be.'

---

[6]The Latin has *ad materiam descendendo.* The sense is that after considering the analogon itself we now proceed to deal with the analogates.

[7]Cf. below, no. 122.

[8]Cf. below, no. 122.

[9]Cf the parallel passage in no. 1 and footnote 4 of Chapter One.

[10]Cf. below, no. 82.

72 I am using the words *in such a way,* because I do not wish to argue at present about the proper names[11] implying these proportions to 'to be' in the order of exercise.[12] For that is the work of a metaphysician, and here we are speaking of being merely as an example. The same rule applies to act, potency, form, matter, principle, cause and other things of this sort.

[11]Such as being, act, principle, etc.

[12]Concerning this expression, see below, footnote 10 of Chapter Seven.

CHAPTER SEVEN

THE DEFINITION OF THE ANALOGATES

Two Difficulties

73 *First Difficulty.* One might also have the impression that in the notion of one analogate (e.g. quality), as expressed by the name of the analogon (e.g. being), the notion of the other analogate (e.g. substance or quantity), as expressed by the same name, ought to be included, just as we said happens in analogy of attribution. This impression is based upon the fact that the notion of one analogate, insofar as it is the same proportionally as the other, cannot be completely expressed without the notion of this other. Now, as has been explained, in the analogous name the notions of the analogates are implied insofar as they are proportionally the same.

74 *Second Difficulty.* This impression may be corroborated by the very treatment of analogy by Aristotle,[1] Averroes[2] and St. Thomas[3] in *I Ethics.* For they explain that *good* or *perfection* is predicated analogically of sight and intelligence because just as sight is a perfection in the body so intelligence is a perfection in the soul. Now it is clear that one cannot understand that this thing is like that thing unless both these extremes are considered. Therefore, it seems that one of the analogates, as expressed by the name of the analogon, must of necessity be defined by means of the other.[4]

75 In order to make clear how this doubt is solved we should keep in mind that analogous terms of this type are found in two ways,

---

[1]*Nic. Ethics* I, 6 (1096b 29f.), quoted above in no. 28.

[2]Cf. footnote 13 of Chapter Three.

[3]Cf. footnote 2 of Chapter Three.

[4]Sylvester of Ferrara in his commentary in *I Contra Gentes,* ch. 34 (IX), says: "One can also answer, and in my opinion this is more in conformity with the mind of St. Thomas, that in every mode of analogy it is true that the primary analogate (*prius*) must be put into the definition of the secondary analogate (*posterius*) insofar as it is considered and signified analogously." Modern Thomists are still divided about this point. Ramirez (*op. cit.* pp. 77ff.), Le Rohellec (*op. cit.* pp. 144ff.), Penido (*op. cit.* pp. 47ff.), and Anderson (*op. cit.* pp. 241ff.) follow Cajetan; Blanche (*"L'analogie,"* in *Revue de philosophie,* 1923, pp. 248ff., *"La notion de l'analogie dans la philosophie de Saint Thomas,"* in *Revue des sciences philosophique et théologique,* 1921, pp. 169ff., etc.) and Balthasar (*L'abstraction métaphysique et l'analogie des êtres dans l'être,* Louvain, 1935) follow Sylvester of Ferrara.

namely, properly and metaphorically. For with respect to the present problem these two types are different.

Definition of the Analogates in Metaphorical Analogy

In analogy by metaphor one analogate must be placed in the notion of the other, not in just any way, but the proper sense must be included in the notion of the analogon taken metaphorically. For it is impossible to understand what something is with respect to a metaphorical name unless that thing is known to which the metaphor refers. For instance, it is not possible for me to understand what a meadow is insofar as it is *smiling* unless I know what the term *smile* means in its proper sense, by similitude to which a meadow is said to smile.

76 The fundamental reason of this is that an analogon, taken metaphorically, predicates nothing else than that this thing bears a likeness to that thing, and this likeness cannot be understood without [knowledge of] the other extreme. For this reason analogous terms of this type are predicated by priority of those things in which they are properly realized, and by posteriority of those in which they are found metaphorically. As is clear, in this respect they resemble terms that are analogous by analogy of attribution.

Definition of the Analogates in Proper Proportionality

77 In analogy in which the proper sense of the name is realized [in each of the analogates] one member of the analogon[5] does not have to be defined by means of the other,[6] unless perhaps because of

---

[5]The *analogates* are the things in which an analogon is realized; the *members of an analogon* are the notions signified by the analogous name as found in the analogates; e.g. substance and quantity are analogates of being, and the notions of being as realized in substance and quantity are the members of the analogon *being*. Cf. no. 97.

[6]Commenting upon the words of St. Thomas: "In all names which are predicated analogously of several, it is necessary that all be spoken of with respect to one thing, and therefore this one thing must be put into the definition of all," Cajetan remarks (in *S. T.* I, 13, 6, III and IV): St. Thomas himself, in *de Veritate* 2, 11, says that it is not universally true that the primary analogate must be put into the notions of the other analogates . . . Briefly, the answer is that analogous names are found in two ways. Some signify the respects themselves to the primary analogate, as is clear in *healthy*. Others, however, signify only the *foundations* of these respects, as commonly is the case in nearly all truly analogous terms, which are properly and formally realized in all analogates. Therefore the universal proposition [in every analogous name there is one to which the others have a respect and therefore this one thing is put into the definition of the others] . . . has to be understood as a universal rule in the first mode of analogy [i.e. analogy of attribution].

matter, as St. Thomas teaches in *de Veritate,* q.2, a. 11.[7] The notions of the analogates, as expressed by the name of the analogon, are in a certain sense midway between what is analogous by attribution and what is univocal. In analogy by attribution the primary [extreme] defines the others,[8] whereas in univocation neither [extreme] defines the other, but the definition of one is the complete definition of the other, and vice versa. But in analogy [of proper proportionality] neither [extreme] defines the other, but the definition of one is proportionally the definition of the other. All the time we are speaking of the notion [of the extremes] as expressed by the common name.

Its sense, therefore, is that in all names which are predicated of several analogously, i.e. according to diverse respects, one thing must be put [into the definition of the others]. But in *de Veritate* [2, 11, St. Thomas] says the opposite with respect to the second mode of analogy [i.e. analogy according to proportionality]. This answer is more general than the one we have given elsewhere [in *de Nominum Analogia,* no. 77], with respect to the question of *de Veritate.* For this answer applies also to terms which are analogous according to proportionality, provided they be used metaphorically, for in these terms, too, one thing is put into the notion of the other, for the reason given above."

[7]Cf. footnote 8 of Chapter Three.

[8]Cf. no. 14. In his commentary in *de Ente et Essentia* (cap. II, q. 3, no. 21, ed. Laurent), Cajetan says: "Analogates are those things whose name is common, and the notion expressed by this name is somewhat the same and somewhat different or the same to a certain extent and different to a certain extent . . . There are two kinds of analogates. Some [things are analogated] according to a *determinate relationship* of one to another, others according to *proportionality.* For example, substance and accident are analogates in the first way, but God and creature in the second because the distance between God and creature is infinite. These two [types of analogates] differ very much. Analogates of the first type are related in such a way that what is posterior with respect to the analogous name is defined by what is prior to it; e.g. accident as a being is defined by substance. The same does not hold for analogates of the second type, for a creature insofar as it is a being not defined by God. Hence analogates of the first type have a common name, and the notion expressed by this name is the same to a certain extent and diverse to a certain extent, for this analogous name, taken absolutely, i.e. without any addition, is predicated of the first, whereas of the others it is predicated only according to their diverse relationships to the first, and this first belongs to their definition, as is clear from the example of health. Analogates of the second type, however, have a common name, and the notion expressed by this name is somewhat the same and somewhat diverse, not because this name is predicated of the first absolutely and of the others relatively to the first, but because they have to a certain extent the same notion because of their proportional identity, and to a certain extent a diverse notion because of the diverse natures which underlie these proportions. For instance, substantial form and matter and the form and matter of accidents are analogated under the names *form* and *matter.* They have a common name (form and matter), and the notion expressed by these names is the same and diverse in this way because the substantial form is related to substance as the accidental form is to accident, and likewise the matter of substance is related to substance as the matter of accident is related to accident: in both cases there is an identity of proportions together with a diversity of natures and a unity of name."

For example, in the definition of the *heart* insofar as it is the *principle* of an animal, we do not put a *foundation* insofar as a foundation is the *principle* of a house, nor vice versa, but the same notion of principle is proportionally in both, as the Commentator says in the text quoted above.[9]

78 *Distinctions to be Made in This Matter.* In this matter it is necessary to make two distinctions—the one which in logic is made between the *order of specification* and the *order of exercise,*[10] and the one which is generally dealt with by the metaphysician between the order of things included under one term with respect to the things [signified] and this order with respect to the imposition of the name.

79 *Consequences of the First Distinction.* From the first distinction we know two things. First of all, since *animal* as predicated of man and horse implies univocation in the order of exercise, it does not predicate of man this whole, "a sensitive nature that is exactly the same in concept as the sensitive nature of a horse or an ox," but it predicates sensitive nature absolutely. Nevertheless, in order to have univocal predication the sensitive nature taken absolutely must be exactly the same in concept as the sensitive nature of a horse or an ox. In the same way, *being* [as predicated of quantity], implies proportionality in the order of exercise and does not predicate of quantity this whole, "something related to 'to be' in the same way as substance or quality is related to its 'to be,'" but it predicates "something related to 'to be' in such a way," without any further addition. Nevertheless, in order to have analogous predication, this "something related to 'to be' in such a way" must be proportionally the same with the other "something related to 'to be' in such a way" which being predicates of substance or quality.

80 Secondly, the explanation showing that *animal* is univocal because it predicates exactly one and the same notion in all does not deceive, confuse or leave us wondering about the nature of man and ox as expressed by the name *animal,* but we are satisfied, seeing that animal

---

[9]Quoted in footnote 13 of Chapter Three.

[10]We shall use these expressions as approximate translations of *in actu signato* and *in actu exercito.* When something is taken *in actu signato,* we consider its nature as it is in itself, without paying attention to the manner in which it is realized concretely. If something is taken *in actu exercito* we consider it as it is realized in a particular instance. Other approximate translations of these terms would be *formally* and *materially, in itself* and *in its particular realizations, taken abstractly* and *taken concretely.*

has in the order of exercise what the definition and explanation of univocals states in the order of specification. In the same way, when *being* or *good* or anything else is declared to be analogous because it expresses several notions that are proportionally the same, and implies that this thing is proportionally related to 'to be' or to the appetite, etc. just like that thing, we must not become disturbed and look for the signate expression of this proportionality in the notion expressed by an analogous name (e.g. *good*). But distinguishing between the order of specification and the order of exercise, we should be satisfied to see that the notion of the analogous name has in the order of exercise what the definition and explanation of the analogon states in the order of specification.

81 From these two observations the conclusion should be evident—namely, that one member of the analogon need not be defined by means of the other just because the analogon signifies that these members are proportionally the same, for it signifies them [merely] in the order of exercise.

82 *Consequences of the Second Distinction.* From the second distinction we know, *in the first place,* that the order of things and significations is sometimes inverse, so that a perfection which is prior in reality is often posterior in being signified. This happens, for example, with *being, good* and such like perfections which are common to God and creatures—the perfection which each of these posits in God is posterior in being signified but prior in reality.[11]

In the second place, because of this posteriority in signification the analogon is said to be predicated of its analogates according to priority and posteriority with respect to the character itself of the analogon.

---

[11]Cf. Cajetan's commentary in *S. T.* I, 13, 6 (X, XII): (X) "When it is said that such common names are predicated by priority of God with respect to the thing signified, this assertion should not be understood materially but formally, so that it has to be verified with respect to the thing formally signified."

(XII) "Although predicated of both formally, the formality in God is prior as regards the thing signified to this formality in the others. Nevertheless it is not prior in the manner in which what defines is prior to what is defined, but it is prior at least in the manner in which the exemplary cause is prior to the copy. For this reason, just as all copies are such with respect to the exemplar, so all creatures are such, say, good, with respect to the divine goodness. And just as there is no need to signify copies in relationship to the exemplar, although they have one, so also is it not necessary to signify the goodness of a creature in relationship to the divine goodness, although in the order of reality they always have a relationship to the exemplar."

In the third place, we know that when the character which the analogon posits in one thing is explained by means of the character which it posits in the other, the reason is not that one belongs to the notion of the other, but that the notion of one is posterior to the other in being signified and is explained by the thing prior because the latter is better known. St. Thomas[12] in *Summa Theologica* I, q. 13, a. 2 gave an example of this when he explains that "when we say, *God is good,* . . . the meaning is, *whatever we call goodness in creatures preexists in God proportionally,*" etc.[13] In the same way the matter must be understood if what is posterior in reality is explained by what is prior.

Therefore, the analogon according to one [particular] notion does not define itself according to the other [particular] notion, although [the latter] explains and clarifies it.

Answer to the Objections

83 Although the objections to the opposite have been satisfactorily answered in the foregoing, by way of a formal answer we may say that there are two ways in which several things are known to be the same proportionally, i.e. that this thing is related just like that thing.

---

[12]The actual text of the *Summa* has: "When it is said that God is good, the sense is not that God is the cause of goodness, or that God is not evil, but that whatever goodness is said to be found in creatures preexists in God, and in a higher mode."

[13]Cf. Cajetan's commentary in *S. T.* I, 13, 6 (VIII-IX): "If *God is good* means *God is causally and formally good,* it follows first that *good* as predicated of God does not signify one thing, which is against Aristotle, in *IV Metaphysics* [III, 2 (996a 22ff.)]. Secondly, this meaning would be opposite to what is intended. For the sense would be *God is the cause of the goodness of others and has goodness in Himself,* so that the goodness of others would manifestly be placed in the definition of God insofar as good.

In reply we may say that these words can be understood indeed in two ways. First, they can be understood as referring to separate possible meanings, i.e. such names can be predicated of and verified in God in both ways, causally and formally, but not jointly. In this case, the proposition *God is good* is true in a causal sense and also in a formal sense, but does not imply both these meanings taken together . . . Secondly, they can be understood as referring to both meanings taken together. In this case, it must be admitted that such names are predicated of God formally, and causally but fundamentally. For example, when it is said that *God is good,* the meaning is not only that *God is one having goodness,* but also that *God has the character of goodness in such a way that it founds the causality of the goodness of others.* In this sense, the words *in such a way* do not add any mode or character to the divine goodness, but are a circumlocution of the formal character by which God is good . . . Although this character does not imply causality, it is its immediate foundation."

In one way, *formally,* i.e. as regards the relationship of identity and similitude; and in this way the knowledge in question cannot be had without [knowledge of] the extremes.

In another way, *fundamentally,* and in this way in the notion of one [extreme] the other is not included, but the notion of the one is the notion of the other adequately or proportionally.

Now it is clear that an analogous name, such as *being* or *good,* does not signify the relationship of identity or similitude [formally] but [only] its foundation. Therefore, the objections, which proceed according to the first sense, conclude nothing against our thesis.

The truth of these assertions can easily be seen if one gives examples of univocal names and considers them with respect to the identity of univocation. For a univocal name signifies several things insofar as they are the same univocally, i.e. with respect to exactly the same notion. And the relationship of identity in neither of the extremes can be understood without [knowledge of] the other.

CHAPTER EIGHT

COMPARISON OF THE ANALOGATES IN THE ANALOGON

A Difficulty

84 We must explain also a major difficulty concerning the comparison [of the analogates] in the analogon which has struck and conquered many. Some believe that once analogy is admitted it will be impossible to explain, except by twisting the point, the statement that one analogate realizes the perfection expressed by the analogous name in a greater or more perfect degree; for example, that substance is more or more perfectly a being than quantity. They are moved by the consideration that a comparison of two extremes must be made in something they have in common, as even the grammarians admit; yet such a common element does not seem to be available in an analogon.

85 The following argument may be given on behalf of this position. Either the analogates are compared in one notion common to them or in their own notions. Now they are not compared in a common notion because an analogon does not have any; nor in their own notions because in this case it is not true that substance is more a being than quantity. For quantity is no less or more imperfectly its own notion which being posits in it than substance is its own, etc. Therefore, it seems that in no way comparision can be reconciled with analogy.

Analogous Comparison is Possible

86 The reason why people fall for this difficulty is that the proper foundation of comparison is not given any consideration. Comparison is founded upon the identity and unity of the thing in which the comparison is made, and not on the mode of identity or unity, just as was explained above with respect to superiority.[1] Since from the preceding chapters it is clear that an analogon expresses a thing which is one, although only proportionally, it follows that nothing

[1]Cf. no. 68.

prevents the analogates from being compared in this, although not in the way it is done in univocal comparison.[2]

87 *Proof.* Three things are required and sufficient for comparison—namely, the distinction of the extremes,[3] the identity of that in which the comparison is made, and the mode in which the identity is realized, i.e. equally or more or less perfectly. Now proportional unity or identity is included under identity or unity. Hence it follows that if in different things a perfection which is proportionally the same has a 'to be' either equally or more or less perfectly, a comparison can be made according to this proportional perfection. This comparison, however, is not univocal but analogical.

88 *Illustration of the Proof.* By univocal comparison a man is said to be more perfectly an animal than an ox, because sensitive nature is in man and in an ox according to exactly the same notion, but has a more perfect 'to be' in man than in an ox. So also by analogical comparison substance is said to be more or more perfectly a being than quantity because "having a reference to 'to be' in such a way" is in substance, and proportionally the same is in quantity, but has a more imperfect 'to be' in quantity than in substance.

St. Thomas' Doctrine of Comparison

In *de Potentia,* q. 7, a. 7, St Thomas[4] explains that there are three modes of comparison and mentions two modes of analogical comparison, thereby obviously suggesting that comparison is based, not only

[2]To Scotus' objection that "every comparison is made in a notion which is somewhat univocal . . . because it is clear that God is a more perfect being than a creature," Cajetan replies in *S. T.* I, 13, 5, X: "Comparison can also be made in an analogon, which is a mean between the univocal and the equivocal, and therefore [Scotus'] assumption must be denied. For when we say, *God is more perfect a being than a creature,* the comparison is made in a notion of being which is one by analogy and thus common to both."

[3]Cf. Cajetan's commentary in II-II, 122, 4, III: "Every comparison is between distinct things and not between a thing and itself."

[4]*ad* 3: *"More* and *less* may be considered in three ways and predicated accordingly. In one way, according to the *quantity alone* of the thing participated; e.g., snow is said to be whiter than a wall because whiteness is more perfect in snow than in a wall, yet it is of the same nature [in both]; hence such a diversity according to *more* or *less* does not diversify the species. In another way, according as one thing is predicated of one *by participation* and of the other *by essence;* e.g., we might say that goodness is better than [a particular] good. In a third way, according as one and the same thing belongs to one *in a more eminent degree* than to another; e.g., heat to the sun and to fire. These two modes prevent unity of species and univocal predication, and it is in this way that something is predicated according to *more* or *less* of God and creature."

upon numerical, specific or generic identity, but also upon proportional identity.

89 *First Mode of Comparison.* The modes of comparison offered in this text are the following. First, according to the quantity alone of the participated perfection. In this way, one white object is said to be whiter than another. If with respect to our present problem we extend this mode to every univocal comparison, we may say that the first mode is had according to the quantity of a participated perfection which is exactly the same in notion, whether this notion be specific or generic; for example, a hot object is said to be hotter than another, and a man is more perfectly an animal than a lion.[5]

90 *Second Mode of Comparison.* The second mode is had insofar as a perfection is found in one thing by participation and in another essentially. For instance, the Platonic man[6] would be far more perfectly a man than we, or taking an example from intellectual abstraction, goodness is far better than any good which is called good by participation.

91 *Third Mode of Comparison.* The third mode is had according as something is found in one thing formally and as such, but in another virtually and raised to a higher order. In this way it is said that the sun is hotter than fire, or that heat has a more perfect 'to be' in the sun than in fire.[7]

92 *Only the First Mode is Univocal.* There is no doubt that these last two modes prevent univocal comparison,[8] as St. Thomas says in the same text.[9] And with respect to the first [of these two], Aristotle

[5]Cf. *S. T.* I-II, 61, 1, *ad* 1: "All animals are equally animals, but they are not all equal animals, for one animal is greater or more perfect than another."

[6]The reference is to the ideal man who exists in the Platonic world of separate ideas.

[7]According to ancient physics, celestial bodies were supposed to be of a more perfect nature than terrestrial bodies. Cf. Joseph de Tonquedec, *op. cit.*, pp. 16ff.

[8]The second mode of comparison, which gives rise to analogy of proper proportionality, applies to perfectly transcendent or absolutely simple perfections, i.e. perfections in whose concept no imperfection is included. The third mode of comparison, which also gives rise to analogy of proper proportionality, applies to imperfectly transcendent or mixed perfections, in whose concept limitation or potentiality is included (e.g. sense-life, man, angel). Such a perfection cannot be found in one essentially and in the other by participation, but may be found according to essentially diverse modes. Cf. Le Rohellec, *op. cit.*, p. 136ff.

[9]Cf. footnote 4 of this Chapter; also *de Potentia*, 7, 7: "A different mode of existing prevents univocal predication. For although the type of the house existing in matter is the same as that of the house in the mind of the architect,

in *I Ethics* [10] testifies to the same when he teaches that *good* must be said to be common to separate goodness and other things which are good by participation, not univocally but by proportionality. From all this it is clear, therefore, that things which are proportionally the same can be compared as such, although physically speaking comparison is made only in species and genus.

Answer to the Objection

93 As regards the objection to the opposite, we say that comparison is made in both ways in analogous terms.[11] The analogates (e.g. substance and quantity), are compared in a notion which is proportionally unified and common and which the name of the analogon (e.g. being) adds to the analogates, as is clear from the foregoing.

The analogates are compared also according to their own notions, yet with respect to the name of the analogon, in order to discover which notion is more perfect. In this way, we say that substance is more perfectly a being than quantity because the notion of being in substance is more perfect than the notion of being in quantity. Thus, according to this comparison the sense is that with respect to the name *being* substance has a more perfect nature than quantity. The sense is not that substance is more perfectly a substance than quantity is quantity, as some seem to imagine.

Comparison of the Analogates in Analogy of Attribution

94 This type of comparison is extended even to terms which are analogous by analogy of attribution, although in such an analogy comparison cannot be made except in an incorrect sense. For instance, we say that real being is more and more perfectly a being than logical being, which, as is said in *IV Metaphysics,*[12] is called being by attribution to real being. For real being has a more perfect nature with respect to the name *being*. In this way, if custom would permit, we would say that an animal is healthier than urine because it has a more perfect nature with respect to the name *health.*

---

since one is the exemplar of the other, nevertheless *house* is not predicated univocally of both because the form of the house has a material 'to be' in matter and an immaterial 'to be' in the mind of the architect."

[10]Ch. 6 (1096b 26ff.), quoted above, in footnote 7 of Chapter One.

[11]i.e. both according to the particular notions of the analogates and according to the notion of the analogon.

[12]Ch. 2 (1003b 6ff.) : "There are many senses in which a thing is said to be, but all refer to one starting-point . . . It is for this reason that we say even of non-being that it *is* non-being."

CHAPTER NINE

DIVISION AND RESOLUTION OF THE ANALOGON

Division of the Analogon

95 *First Division.* How an analogon must be divided will become clear from the following. The division of an analogon can be understood in three ways. First, the *external word* is divided into its *significations.* As has been explained above,[1] an analogous name directly signifies several notions, and this division pertains to it insofar as it is a kind of equivocal term.

96 *Second Division.* Secondly, an analogon is divided when *that which is signified* by it is divided, as it were, into *its members,* insofar as things which are proportionate in this way and in that way can be called members of that which is proportionally one. For, as has been explained,[2] an analogous name does not signify diverse notions without signifying a notion that is proportionally one, because all notions directly signified by an analogous name are proportionally the same. Now since a notion which is proportionally one is composed of several proportional notions, it can be divided into them.

However, this division is not one of an analogon into its analogates. For these proportional notions are intrinsically contained in the very notion of the analogon, whereas the analogates are the things in which these notions are realized but are not these notions themselves. For instance, analogates of *being* are substance and quantity, but not the notions of being in substance and quantity. These notions, as was said, are analogous.

97 *Third Division.* Hence, in a third way, an analogon can be divided by the division of *that which is signified by it* into *its analogates* according to the diverse modes in which the analogates diversely receive the proportional character of the analogon. Thus what is divided is the thing signified, which is proportionally one, and the divisors are the modes which found and establish in the analogates the proper proportions according to which analogy arises. That which is

[1]Cf. no. 32ff.
[2]Cf. no. 56.

constituted by the division as its subjective parts are the analogates themselves.

For example, when *being* is divided into substance and quantity, the thing divided is the nature signified by the name *being,* and this nature includes in itself all the natures signified by the term *being* inasmuch as it is proportionally one. The divisors are *substantive* and *mensurative,* i.e. *in itself* and *in another,* as [the foundations] from which substance and quantity take on diverse modes of being. The subjective parts are substance and quality, which are analogated in the notion of being.

Differences Between Univocal and Analogous Division

98 Because this last division is the proper division of an analogon, it has to be clearly explained how this division differs from a univocal division. These two types of division differ in three ways.

First Difference. First, on the part of *the thing divided.* For in a univocal division there is a division of something which is absolutely one in nature, whereas in this division the thing divided is one proportionally.

99 *Second Difference.* Secondly, on the part of the *divisors.* For the differences which divide a genus are outside the genus,[3] whereas the modes dividing the analogon are included in the notion of the analogon itself, as are also the analogates, as was explained in the chapter on abstraction.[4] For this reason it is denied in *III Metaphysics*[5] that being is a genus.

100 *Third Difference.* Thirdly, with respect to the *subjective parts* themselves which arise from the division. The parts of a univocal division have an order among themselves both with respect to origin (as duality is prior to trinity) and with respect to perfection (as

---

[3]Cf. St. Thomas, *de Potentia,* 3, 16, *ad* 4: "*Being* is not related to what is contained under it in the same way as *animal* or any other genus is related to its species. For a species adds to the genus something which is outside the essence of the genus; e.g. man adds [something] to animal. For *animal* expresses only sensitive nature, in which *rational* is not contained, whereas the things contained under being do not add to being anything which is outside its essence."

[4]Cf. no. 47.

[5]Ch. 3 (998a 21): "But it is not possible that either unity or being should be a single genus of things."

white is more perfect than black).[6] However, with respect to the notion of the thing divided (e.g. number or color) neither is prior or posterior to the other, but all communicate equally in the notion of the thing divided.

On the other hand, the analogates, which are constituted by an analogous division, have an order not only among themselves, but also in the notion of the analogon itself which is divided. One analogate is prior and the other is posterior in such a way that in one of the analogates the character of the divided [analogon] is said to be realized in its entirety, but in the other imperfectly or to a certain extent.[7]

This assertion, however, must not be understood as if the analogon has one notion which is realized totally in one [analogate] and only partially in another. *Totally* is the same as *perfectly,* and the analogous name implies many characters of which one simply and perfectly constitutes the character expressed by the analogous term, whereas the others consitute it imperfectly and only to a certain extent. Therefore, we may say that an analogon is so divided that its whole notion is not realized in all the analogates, and that they do not equally participate in the notion of the analogon, but according to priority and posteriority.[8]

---

[6]According to ancient physics different colors are produced by different mixtures of white, which has the most light, and black, which has the least. Hence white was considered the most perfect of all colors. Cf. Tonquedec, *op. cit.,* pp. 88ff.

[7]Cf. St. Thomas, in *II Sentent.* 42, 1, 3: "There are two ways of dividing a common [notion] into its inferiors, just as there are two modes of having something in common. [First,] there is the division of the *univocal* into species by means of differences by which the generic nature is equally participated in the species. In this way, *animal* is divided into man, horse, etc. Secondly, there is the division of what is *common by analogy.* This common element is predicated according to its perfect character of one of the divisors, but imperfectly and to a certain extent only of the other; as *being* is divided into substance and accident, and into being in act and being in potency. This division is, as it were, a mean between the equivocal and the univocal." And *S. T.* I, 5, 6, *ad* 3: "The *good* is not divided into these three [the disinterested, the pleasant and the useful] as a univocal which is equally predicated of them, but as an analogon which is predicated according to priority and posteriority, for it is predicated by priority of the disinterested good, secondarily of the pleasant, and thirdly of the useful."

[8]I.e. according to a higher or lesser degree or unequally, as is clear from the preceding paragraphs. Hence there is no question of an order of dependence, as is the case in analogy of attribution, but of inequality in the very way a common perfection is formally possessed.

Cf. St. Thomas, *de Malo,* 7, 1, *ad* 1: "Another division is that by which the analogously common is divided into those things of which it is predicated by priority and posteriority, as *being* is divided by substance and accident, and by potency and act. In such cases the common nature is perfectly realized in

101 The assertion that the analogon is realized simply in one analogate and only to a certain extent in another must be taken with a grain of salt. It is sufficient that this be true either [absolutely or relatively. The first, i.e.] *absolutely,* is evidenced in the division of *being* into substance and accident, for, absolutely speaking, substance is called a being simply, whereas an accident is called a being to a certain extent. [The second, i.e.] *relatively,* is evidenced in the division of *being* into God and creatures. For although absolutely speaking, both are and should be called being simply, nevertheless a creature in relation to God is a being only to a certain extent; it is and is called, as it were, a non-being.

Resolution of the Analogates

102 With regard to the resolution of the analogates, the following should be kept in mind.[9] Universally, what is first in composition is last in resolution, and resolution is made by the division of a thing into its actual constituent parts. Hence analogates must be resolved into their analogon in the same manner in which other [extremes] are resolved—namely, by the use of the above-mentioned division, which is called the division into essential or notional parts, and by an orderly procedure from things posterior to things prior if a long resolution has to be made.

---

one, but in the others only to a certain extent and by posteriority." *S. T.* I-II, 61, 1, *ad* 1: "When a *univocal* is divided into its species, the members of the division are on a par with respect to the generic notion, although in the order of reality one species may be higher ranking and more perfect than another, e.g. man with respect to other animals. When however, an *analogon* is divided, which is predicated of several by priority and posteriority, there is nothing to prevent one from being prior to the other even with respect to the common notion, as *being* is predicated of substance more principally than of accident." In his commentary on this text Cajetan remarks, "Take note, philosopher, of the answer to the first objection, and you will see how well we have written elsewhere about the analogy of names."

Cf. also St. Thomas, in *I Perihermeneias,* lect. 8: "In two ways something common may belong prior to one than to another of its divisors. In one way, according to the *proper notions* or natures of the divisors. In another way, according to their participation in that *common notion* which is divided into them. The first way does not prevent univocation as a genus, as is clear in numbers. For according to its proper notion two is prior to three; nevertheless they participate equally in their generic notion, i.e., number; for just as three is a multitude numbered by one, so also two. But the second way prevents univocation as a genus, and therefore *being* cannot be the genus of substance and accident because in the very notion of *being* substance, which is a being *by* and *in* itself, has priority with respect to accident, which is a being *by* and *in* another."

[9]For an example of resolution, see *The Concept of Being,* no. 8.*

103 When the notion of the analogon has been reached, i.e. after the resolution of each of the analogates into its own notion with respect to the name expressing the analogon, [the process continues as follows.] Since the notion of the analogon is constituted by many notions which have an order to one another and a proportional similitude, *either* we make a resolution in orderly fashion towards the prime notion by approaching steadily towards something more similar and leaving behind that in which there is dissimilitude, *or* if it happens that the notions are not so ordered to one another, we must reduce them all to the prime notion in the above-mentioned manner. For none of the notions can escape having a relationship to the prime notion. As regards the present question, it does not matter whether the resolution is made into the notion which is first in the order of signification or in the order of reality. For these assertions should be understood in their own order, namely, either of significations or of reality.

CHAPTER TEN

REASONING AND ANALOGOUS NAMES*

Two Difficulties

104 *First Difficulty.* Some have the impression that the analogon cannot be known except in the way equivocals are known because it implies several, though similar, notions. More than that, for the same reason they argue that a fallacy of equivocation is committed in syllogisms in which an analogon is taken as the middle term and a definite analogate is used in the minor, although perhaps the process could be valid materially.

Second Difficulty. They also assert that from the notion of one analogate, as expressed by the name of the analogon, one cannot conclude that the other analogate formally realizes the same notion, but that for the same reason one will always fall in the above-mentioned fallacy.

105 For example, if we assert that wisdom is analogically common to God and man in virtue of the fact that wisdom as found in man, taken precisely according to its formal concept, indicates a simple perfection, we cannot conclude that therefore God is formally wise, by arguing in the following manner:

Every simple perfection is in God.
Wisdom is a simple perfection.
Therefore, [wisdom is in God].

For the minor must be distinguished. If the word *wisdom* stands for the character of wisdom as it is in man, the argument has four terms; for in the conclusion wisdom stands for the character of wisdom as it is found in God when we conclude that there is wisdom in God. On the other hand, if in the minor wisdom represents the character of wisdom as it is in God, then the conclusion that God is wise is not drawn from the perfection of created wisdom; yet all
106 philosophers and theologians assert the opposite. This is the argument given by Scotus.[1]

*The Latin has: How there can be science of the analogons.
[1]Art. 4 (Quaracchi ed. 1912, vol. I, no. 346, p. 310).

How an Analogous Name Can be Used in Reasoning

Those who follow Scotus in this argument are deceived. While paying attention to the diversity of notions in the analogon; they fail to consider whatever unity and identity lies hidden in it. For, as was explained above,[2] the notions of the analogon can be taken in two ways.

In one way, *in themselves,* insofar as they are distinguished from one another and according to what pertains to them as such, i.e. insofar as they are distinct.

In another way, insofar as they are *the same proportionally.* Used in the first way, it is obvious that they would lead to the error of equivocation. By using them in the second way, however, one does not commit any fault, because whatever belongs to one belongs also to the other proportionally, and whatever is denied of the one is also denied of the other proportionally. The reason is that whatever pertains to a similar object as such pertains also to that to which it is similar,[3] proportionality of course being always duly observed.

107 Therefore, if from the immateriality of the soul one concludes that it is intellectual, from immateriality proportionally posited in God one could very well conclude that God is proportionally intellectual, i.e. to the degree that His immateriality exceeds that of man, His intellectuality exeeds that of man, etc. For this reason St. Thomas, in *de Potentia,* q. 2, a. 5,[4] says that all analogates fall under the same distribution of the analogon; and rightly so, because unity of analogy could not be classified among unities unless proportional unity would be unity which can be affirmed or denied, and consequently distributed and known as subject, middle term and predicate.

Solution of the First Difficulty

108 In answer to the objections it can be said that, as is stated in *II Sophistical Refutations,*[5] Ch. X, the equivocation hidden in propor-

---

[2]Cf. above, no. 70.

[3]Cf. Cajetan's *The Concept of Being* (in appendix, no. 3*).

[4]*Ad* 6: "The generation of the Son and the production of creatures do not fall under one notion by univocation but only by analogy. For Basilius says that *to receive* is common to the Son and creatures, and for this reason He is called the *First-Born of All Creatures,* and in this way His generation may be joined to the productions of creatures under the distribution of one notion."

[5]Ch. 33 (182b 13ff.): "In fallacies that depend on ambiguity . . . some are clear even to the man in the street . . .while others appear to elude the most

tional terms of this type escapes even the experts; hence the mode of proportionality must always be kept in mind when these analogous terms are used insofar as they are unified. Otherwise one would fall into univocation. For instance, unless proportionality is kept in mind when it is said that whatever is immaterial is intellectual, this statement would be taken in a univocal sense, and the hidden equivocation would creep [into the argument] unseen.

109 That there can be scientific knowledge of the analogous if due attention is given to proportionality, is convincingly demonstrated by St. Thomas' reasoning concerning the good, the true, etc.,[6] and also by its daily use.

Aristotle, also, the Father of the art of demonstration, in *II Posterior Analytics,*[7] declares that the analogon is the adequate cause of some property and must sometimes be assumed by a demonstrator as a middle term, when teaching how to search for causes he says: "Again, another method is to make a selection by analogy. For we cannot find a single identical [name] which can be used as the name of a squid's pounce, a spine and a bone. Nevertheless, certain [properties] flow from it as if one such nature existed."[8] And in the following chapter he says: "Whatever belongs to the same by analogy is the middle by analogy."[9] In these words he not only taught that the analogon is sometimes used as a middle term in demonstrations, but also states explicitly that it is not *one* in itself, and that notwithstanding this it has a property corresponding to it as if it had one nature.

---

expert." Cf. also *ibid.*, ch. 6 and 7 (168b, 5ff., 169a 22ff.): "It is, however, just in this that the experts and men of science generally suffer refutation at the hand of the unscientific . . . The deception comes about in the case of arguments that depend on ambiguity of words or of phrases because we are unable to divide the ambiguous term (for some terms are not easy to divide, e.g. 'unity,' 'being,' and 'sameness')."

[6]Cf. St. Thomas in *IV Metaphysics,* lect. 1, no. 537, in *I Ethics,* lect. 7, no. 93ff., *de Veritate,* 2, 11 *ad* 5.

[7]The text adds: "Ch. XIII, which begins as follows: In order to have questions or problems."

[8]The modern text, as translated in the Ross' edition, has: "Yet a further method of selection is by analogy; for we cannot find a single identical name to give to a squid's pounce, a fish's spine, and an animal's bone, although these too possess common properties as if they were a single ossuous nature." *Posterior Analytics,* II, 14 (98a 20f.).

[9]The modern text, as translated in the Ross' edition, has: "Again, connexions requiring proof which are identical by analogy have middles also analogous." *Posterior Analytics,* II, 17 (99a 16).

Solution of the Second Difficulty

110 This analogy does not prevent a formal process of reasoning leading to the conclusion that God and creatures have some predicate in common. One can take the notion of wisdom and separate from it by means of the intellect whatever is imperfect. From the fact that what is proper to wisdom, taken formally, implies perfection without any imperfection, the conclusion can be drawn that the character of wisdom in God is not entirely diverse nor entirely the same, but the same proportionally, because the similitude between God and creature is not univocal but analogous.

111 On the other hand, we cannot conclude by a similar argument that God is a stone proportionally.[10] For formally considered the character of a stone, no matter how purified, includes some imperfection, which prevents that character, whether in an absolute sense or proportionally, from being found in God, except metaphorically, in the sense in which it is said that: "The rock was Christ."[11]

Conclusion

Consequently, in a process of reasoning like the following:

Every simple perfection is in God
Wisdom is a simple perfection
Therefore, [wisdom is in God],

the word *wisdom* in the minor does not stand for this or that notion of wisdom, but for wisdom which is proportionally one, i.e. for both notions of wisdom, not taken in conjunction nor in disjunction, but insofar as they are undivided proportionally, insofar as one is the other proportionally, and insofar as both constitute a notion which is proportionally one.

112 Both are signified by the analogous term insofar as they are the same. Hence it is not necessary to distinguish the analogon in order

[10] In his commentary on *S. T.* I, 13, 5 (X), Cajetan says: "Metaphysical arguments begin their inquiry with a notion that is absolutely one, but they end with a notion that is one not absolutely but by analogy. For it is in this way that the notion is one when it is stripped of imperfections. Hence one cannot reason, as Scotus objects, in a like manner with respect to a stone and wisdom. For neither at the beginning nor at the end of the inquiry does the notion of stone remain one by analogy and formally realized in God and a stone because the notion of stone always implies imperfection." Cf. also his commentary in *de Ente et Essentia, cap. II,* (q. 3, no. 19, *tertio sic,* and 21a, *ad tertium*).

[11] *I Cor.* X, 4.

to make it serve as the basis of a contradiction and become the subject or predicate of a proposition. Of its very nature it can do this, in virtue of the proportional identity which is included in it and which it principally expresses.

For contradiction is said to consist in the affirmation and negation of one and the same [predicate]of one and the same [subject], etc., and not in the affirmation and negation of a univocal [predicate] of one and the same univocal [subject]. For, as was repeated so often, identity, both of things and of their notions, extends also to proportional identity.

Reply to Scotus

113 From the foregoing it is clear that Scotus[12] in *I Sentent.*, d. 3, q. 1, either badly explained the univocal concept, or contradicted himself when he wanted to establish the univocation of being and said: "I call univocal a concept which is one in such a way that its unity is sufficient to render contradictory the affirmation and negation of this concept with respect to the same thing." In this sense he claims being to be univocal.[13] But if identity which is sufficient for contradiction is made the definition of univocation, then it is clear that, by stating that being is analogous and unified merely by proportion, one will fulfill the definition of univocation. This, however, is contrary to Scotus' doctrine which maintains that being has a concept that is absolutely *one* and wholly undivided, just as we have explained with respect to univocal terms.

On the other hand, if not just any such identity is sufficient for unification, then it was not correct to say that the univocation of a concept is univocation which is sufficient for contradiction, as if proportional identity were not sufficient for it.

[12]Cf. *loc. cit.* (footnote 1), p. 309.

[13]For a detailed refutation of Scotus' viewpoint by Cajetan, see his commentary in *de Ente et Essentia, cap.* II, q. 3, nos. 19-21a).

CHAPTER ELEVEN

PRECAUTIONS TO BE TAKEN IN THE UNDERSTANDING AND USE OF ANALOGOUS TERMS

Introduction

114 In the above-mentioned text of *Sophistical Refutations*[1] Aristotle says that even very learned men err as regards the concepts of these names because their mode of unity is hidden. For this reason we have deemed it necessary, at the end of this treatise, to indicate certain precautions which will enable one to guard himself from many errors in this matter.

The Origin of a Name and Its Analogous Meaning

115 First of all, we must beware lest from the univocation of an analogous name with respect to certain things we are led to think that this name is univocal in an absolute sense. Almost all analogous names[2] first were univocal and then by extension were rendered analogous, i.e. common by proportion to those things in which they are univocal and to others or to another.[3]

For example, the name *wisdom* was at first given to human wisdom and was univocal to the wisdoms of all men. Then, when men rose to a knowledge of the divine nature and saw the proportional similitude between us insofar as we are wise and God, they extended the name *wisdom* to signify in God that to which our wisdom is proportional. In this way what was univocal to us was made analogous to us and God. The same is true of other terms.

---

[1]Cf. footnote 5 of Chapter Ten.

[2]Like John of St. Thomas, *Logica* II, 13, 3 and 14, 2 (Reiser ed. of the *Cursus Philosophicus,* vol. I, pp. 485, 2f. and 511, 1f.), Cajetan speaks of the univocity of being as predicated of individuals of the same species. In his commentary on *S. T.* I, 13, 5 (XVII), he says: "Being itself, which is predicated by analogy of man and white, is resolved into itself as *univocally* predicated of men and as *univocally* predicated also of white things." Cf. also his commentary in *de Ente et Essentia,* cap. 2, (q. 3, no. 20 in Laurent edition): "These assertions do not prevent being from belonging to the notion of substance as a *univocal* and quidditative predicate." Hence it would seem that James F. Anderson (*op. cit.,* p. 320, footnote 12) uses the wrong argument to prove that Cajetan's doctrine of analogy is more metaphysical than that of John of St. Thomas.

[3]Cf. footnote 10 of Chapter Ten, and no. 3* of *The Concept of Being.*

116 For this reason it is easy to fall into error. The first meaning is better known, more familiar, and prior as regards us; hence eminent scholars and their followers always mention it when one inquires about the meaning of an analogous term. They say that this first meaning is the whole notion of the analogon,[4] that, used absolutely, it stands for this whole notion, and that all the analogates participate in it, as is clear when the notion of wisdom is explained. The differential concept of wisdom is indicated as the notion according to which wisdom is considered common to God and creatures.[5]

The same goes for other [analogous notions]. As a result, some are led to believe that this notion is the very notion of the analogon, and imprudently univocation is accepted. However, this notion is not the notion of the analogon, but its origin as regards us. For it is not this notion [absolutely], but this notion proportionally which is found in the other analogate, as is clear from the foregoing.

Unity and Diversity of Names and Analogy

117 The second precaution to take is to beware lest the unity or diversity of name render obscure the analogous unity of the notions.[6] In this matter unity or diversity of name should be considered as something accidental.

For instance, although a squid's pounce, a bone and a spine do not have one name, they are no less analogously similar than if they had one name. Nor would they be more similar if they had one name. Nevertheless, if they were called *bones* by a common name in such a way that through lack of words or because of their proportional similitude the name *bone* were extended to the others, we would believe bones, squid's pounce and spine to be of the same nature and notion. Especially, because, as was explained above,[7] certain proportions flow from things which are proportionally the same as if they had one nature.

---

[4]Cf. St. Thomas, *S. T.* I, 33, 3; "A name is predicated of that in which its whole notion is perfectly realized before it is predicated of that in which it is realized only to a certain extent."

[5]Cf. above, nos. 110f. and *The Concept of Being,* no. 5.*

[6]The Zammit-Hering edition punctuates as follows: *ne nominis unitas, aut diversitas rationum, analogam unitatem obnubilet.* The context however, shows that the puntuation should be: *ne nominis unitas aut diversitas, rationum analogam unitatem obnubilet.*

[7]Cf. above, no. 109.

Unity of Names and Univocity

118 The third precaution to take is to beware lest the vocal unity of the notion expressed by an analogous term confuse the mind.

For instance, a *principle* is said to be that from which a thing comes to be, is, or is known, and this definition is realized in everything called a principle. Hence the term *principle* is thought to be univocal. Nevertheless, this is wrong because this very definition is not unified absolutely, but only proportionally and as regards the external term. The words from which it is formed are analogous, as is clear. Neither *to come to be,* nor *to be,* nor *to be known,* nor *from which* has exactly the same meaning, but is realized proportionally. This is the reason why this notion is realized in all [analogates] insofar as proportional, just like the name *principle* is said to be common proportionally.

Apparently Contradictory Teachings of Philosophers

119 Finally, we must beware lest the different statements of scholars concerning analogous terms confuse us. It should be kept in mind that the analogous is a mean between the univocal and the equivocal, and that the mean partakes of the nature of both extremes. Hence when it is compared to one extreme, it takes on the appearance of the other extreme, to such an extent that, when we make use of the mean insofar as it agrees with one extreme, we attribute to it the conditions of this extreme, as is clear from *V Physics.*[8]

For this reason most scholars, when using an analogous term under the aspect of the unity which it shares with univocal terms, attribute to it not only the conditions of univocal terms, such as abstraction, indistinction, etc., but also the name. On the other hand, when they use an analogous term under the aspect of the diversity which it takes from equivocal terms, they attribute to it also the conditions opposed to those mentioned above [for univocals] and call it equivocal.

120 *Examples of Analogous Terms Used Under the Aspect of Unity.* To give a few examples among many, Aristotle in *II Metaphysics*[9]

[8]Ch. 1 (224b 32ff.): "The intermediary is in a sense the extremes. Hence we speak of the intermediate as a contrary relatively to the extremes and of either extreme as a contrary relatively to the intermediate: for instance, the central note is low relatively to the highest and high relatively to the lowest, and grey is light relatively to black and dark relatively to white." Ch. 5 (229b 20): "The middle is opposed in a sense to either of the extremes." Cf. St. Thomas, in *V Physics,* lect. 1 and lect. 7, and *S. T.* I, 50, 1, *ad* 1.

[9]Ch. 2 (993b 22ff.) "Now we do not know a truth without its causes; and a thing has a quality in a higher degree than other things if in virtue of

calls being and truth univocal because he considers them under the aspect of identity, as is clearly shown by his way of reasoning.

St. Thomas, also, says several times that in the notion of some analogous terms, such as *paternity,* which is common to divine and human paternity, everything is contained undivided and indistinct, and that e.g. paternity abstracts from human and divine paternity.[10] He uses the analogous term with respect to identity.

121 However, these and other similar expressions of both men are not false or incorrect, but rather broad and used in a wide sense, in the same way as pale is said to be the contrary of black. For in analogous terms the identity of name and notion is safeguarded, and, as is clear from the foregoing, in this identity not only the analogates but also each of the notions of the analogon are united and in some way confused inasmuch as they abstract somehow from their diversity.

122 *Examples of Analogous Terms Used Under the Aspect of Diversity.* Again, Aristotle, the Father [of Logic], in *I Physics,* used *being* from the viewpoint of diversity against Parmenides and Melissus, and called it multiple or equivocal.[11] In *II Sophistical Refutations*[12] he himself explicitly states that this text must be understood in this way. From this text Porphyry,[13] too, seems to have taken the view

---

it a similar quality belongs to the other things as well (e.g. fire is the hottest of things; for it is the cause of the heat of all other things); so that that which causes derivative truths to be true is most true. Hence the principles of eternal things must always be most true (for they are not merely sometimes true nor is there any cause of their being, but they themselves are the cause of the being of other things), so that as each thing is in respect of being, so it is in respect of truth." The ancient Latin version has: *Unumquodque vero maxime id ipsum aliorum dicitur secundum quod in aliis inest univocatio.* ("The same predicate is attributed to any thing in a higher degree than to others if in virtue of it this predicate is in the others univocally."). Cf. St. Thomas, in *II Metaphysics,* lect. 2, nos. 292ff.

[10]Cf. St. Thomas, *S. T.* I, 33, 3.

[11]Ch. 2 (185a 20ff.): "The most pertinent question with which to begin will be this: In what sense is it asserted that all things *are* one? For 'is' is used in many senses." Ch. 3 (186a 24f.): "[Parmenides'] assumption that one is used in a single sense only is false because it is used in several." Cf. also *ibid.,* 3 (187a 1ff.)

[12]Ch. 32 (182b 25ff.): "Some think 'Being' and 'One' mean the same, while others solve the argument of Zeno and Parmenides by asserting that 'One' and 'Being' are used in a number of senses."

[13]"If one calls all things beings, [Aristotle] says, one will be speaking equivocally, not univocally." In his commentary on this text (*in Porphyrii Isagogen,* Rome, 1934, p. 52), Cajetan remarks: "If being were the common genus of all things, it would be univocal. Being, however, is not univocal, because Aristotle says that if one calls all things beings, one will be speaking equivocally, and because the univocal is common in name and in the notion expressed by this name, whereas being is common only in name and not in notion."

that according to Aristotle *being* is equivocal.[14] He uses *being* under the aspect of its diversity. Scotus, however, in *I Sentent.*, dist. 3, q.3, said that this is not found in the Logic of Aristotle[15] because he did not consider together the above-mentioned texts. Thus he was led, in the same work,[16] to comment upon the principle used by Aristotle against Parmenides in *I Physics*,[17] in a way which goes against the text, as is clearly evident from the above-mentioned text in *Sophistical Refutations*.[18]

23 St. Thomas,[19] also, says several times that *being* is not prior to the primary analogate and that nothing is prior in concept to God. He uses the analogous term under the aspect of the diversity of its notions. Each notion of the analogon, taken in itself, includes in itself its own analogate, and in its abstraction draws this analogate with it; hence it is convertible with it, as was explained above.[20] Therefore, it is denied that it is prior in the order of succession or more abstract than its own analogate. For this reason nothing is prior to the primary analogate and God, for the notion of God, as expressed by the name of the analogon, in itself is not prior to Him but convertible, yet it is prior to the other notions.

24 Nevertheless, as is clear from the foregoing, this notion in God, insofar as it is proportionally the same as the other notion, is superior with respect to the same name and, logically speaking, prior in the order of succession. I say *logically*, because, *physically* speaking, the analogon is not prior in succession to all the analogates. For it cannot abstract from their proper notions, although in order to be realized in one it should be prior to the other. Nor can it be without a primary analogate if the analogates have an order of succession.

Conclusion

25 If one does not want to fall into error, he should diligently look for the purpose of the expressions and remember that he is going

---

14Cf. *Categories* 1 (1a 1ff.), quoted in footnote 21 of Chapter Two.

15a. 2 (Quaracchi ed. vol. I, 1912, no. 386 p. 346).

16In *I Sentent.* d. 3, q. 3 a. 2, no. 386, p. 346. Cf. footnote 13 of Chapter Ten.

17Cf. footnote 11 of this Chapter.

18Cf. footnote 12 of this Chapter.

19*Contra Gentes* I, 32: "What is univocally predicated of several is simpler than both of them, at least in concept. But nothing can be simpler than God, whether in reality or in concept. Therefore, nothing can be predicated of God and other things in a univocal sense."

20Cf. above, no. 70.

to apply the conditions of the extremes to the middle. In this way it will be easy to explain everything correctly and attain to the truth, which comes from the First Truth.

May Its knowledge be exalted and rendered more solid by this little work.

Completed in the convent of St. Apollinaris, in the suburbs of Pavia, first day of September, 1498.

APPENDIX

THE CONCEPT OF BEING

An Answer to Two Questions of Fr. Francis of Ferrara Concerning the Concept of Being

Introduction

1* Dear Father,

From the letter received through your care, I perceive that you and your confreres have carefully read our treatise *The Analogy of Names,* and that there remain in your minds two doubts concerning the concept of being, which you kindly beg me to solve.

As soon as I had completed the exposition of the book *On the Soul,*[1] to which I was giving the finishing touches when I received your letter, I have taken care to answer in order not to disappoint your keen mind.

Two Doubts

2* *First Doubt.* The first doubt concerns myself personally—namely, that in the commentary on *Being and Essence*[2] I maintain that there

---

[1]February 25, 1509. Cf. J. F. Groner, *Kardinal Cajetan,* Fribourg-Louvain, 1951, p. 68.

[2]Ch. I (q. 2, no. 14 in Laurent edition): "That *being* signifies one formal concept which is the common representation of substance and accident, God and creature . . . is proved in this way. All things which are similar by any similitude whatsoever, even analogous or imitative similitude, can be represented by the same image, with respect to that in which they are similar. Now God and creatures, substance and accident, have at least an analogous similitude to one another. Therefore, with respect to that in which they are similar, they can be represented by the same similitude, insofar as they have a 'to be.' Now this similitude is the formal concept of being. Therefore, etc.

The argument is clear, and the propositions are admitted by all when the major premise is explained. This premise may be made acceptable from better known propositions in the following way. Whenever an agent is found to produce its likeness in another, and this other produces a third which is similar to the first, of necessity the third must be similar to both, because whatever is similar to a thing with respect to that in which this thing is similar to a third is similar to both . . . Now it is in this way that in things having an analogous similitude (God and creature, substance and accident) such a relationship is found with respect to the formal concept [of being]; therefore, etc. . .

is one mental concept which represents being, while in the treatise *The Analogy of Names*[3] I seem to deny this.

Second Doubt. The second doubt concerns St. Thomas. In the above-mentioned treatise I hold that the analogon is not abstracted from those things to which it is said to be analogous.[4] St. Thomas, however, in *de Veritate,* q.1, a.1,[5] teaches that being has one simple concept, to which all the predicaments and transcendentals add [something], into which they are resolved, and which is the first known. It seems that these two opinions are opposed to one another. For if being cannot be abstracted from the natures of things, it will not be the most simple concept, nor the first known, nor the concept into which resolution is ultimately made and to which all others add [something].

Solution of the First Doubt

3* To settle these doubts, and especially the first one, you should recall that whatever is an image of something similar to another is also the image of this third thing insofar as it is similar to the first.[6] In this way, every concept of a creature is a concept of God, just as every creature is a kind of likeness of God. This is the reason why what is proportionably *one* and therefore as such has members, each of which is similar proportionably, must also have one mental concept which represent this proportionably one thing.

4* I do not hold the opposite of this in the treatise *The Analogy of Names.* This concept which is numerically *one* in the mind, in the

---

There is no need to posit several concepts and to multiply beings without necessity. This explanation is not only in accordance with the mind of Saint Thomas, but also with his explicit views, as is clear from the *Disputed Question, de Potentia,* [7, 5], from which I have taken this proof, and also from the same question, near the end [art. 6].

Cf. also *ibid.* (no. 21 in Laurent edition): "When *being* is predicated of God and creature it is predicated in this way, proportionably, by which is expressed that just as God is related to His 'to be,' so a creature is related to its 'to be.' . . . For the present these few words should be sufficient to make clear that the formal concept of being is one and unequally represents the 'to be' of substance and accident, of God and creature, and that the objective concept has nothing but the unity of a proportion determined by identity of term or by unity of proportionability and identity of proportions."

[3]Cf. above, no. 36.

[4]Cf. above, no. 47.

[5]"That which the intellect first conceives as the most known and into which it resolves all its concepts is being . . . Hence it follows that all other concepts of the intellect are obtained by an addition to being."

[6]Cf. above, nos. 36 and 106.

subjective order, is *one* by analogy in the order of representation. It does not represent only one nature, but apart from the one which it represents determinately—the one by which it is impressed [in the intellect]—it signifies implicitly the others that are similar to the one first represented, with respect to that in which it is proportionably similar to them.[7] For the same judgment applies to the similitude of things to one another, and to the similitude of mental concepts to things.

For instance, just as the nature of *bone* is similar to that of the *spine* in sustaining the flesh of animals (in this spine and bone are analogated), so the mental concept of bone as sustaining flesh is similar to bone and spine, but to bone determinately and to spine implicitly, just as also the bone itself is not similar to the spine in a determinate way, but only insofar as the spine sustains flesh just as the bone does.

This is the *first* way in which the analogon has one mental concept. Hence since *being* is analogous, by the same token, it has one mental concept impressed upon the mind by reality.

5* The *second* way is based upon the working of the intellect itself, whose nature it is to divide what is united. In this case there is a similar concept which is numerically *one* and which represents the analogon determinately, without, however, explicitly representing any of those things which give rise to the analogy. This happens when the intellect strips the mental concept, referred to above, of the determinate nature which it represented and in place of this nature conceives some pronoun which refers indeterminately to the natures giving rise to analogy.

For example, if the concept of *bone* is *bone sustaining flesh,* the intellect replaces *bone* by *that which is* and says *that which sustains flesh.* Thus the analogon is manifestly represented explicitly, but the natures which gave rise to the analogy are represented only implicitly.

6* Between these two concepts there is not only the above-mentioned difference of origin, but also this other—the first concept is concerned with the nature of the reality represented by the analogon, whereas the second is concerned with what is expressed by the name. Neither, however, perfectly represents the analogon. Whenever it is found

[7]The Zammit edition has: *in quo proportionabiliter ei similis est.* To make sense it should be either *in quo proportionabiliter eis similis est,* or *in quo proportionabiliter ei similes sunt.* The first correction was selected because it requires a minimum of change.

written by me or anyone else that the analogon cannot have a mental concept which is numerically *one,* but only a concept which is *one* by analogy, it must be interpreted as referring to the perfect and adequate concept of the analogon.

Solution of the Second Doubt

7* Unless they are fictitious, mental concepts are images of things represented. Therefore, just as in the mind the adequate concept of the analogon is not *one,* but necessarily represents all those things which gave rise to the analogy, so also the perfect and adequate character signified by the analogon cannot be abstracted in such a way that it becomes an object of the intellect, or is represented or conceived without the things that gave rise to it. And just as in the mind a twofold imperfect concept is found, so the thing signified can become the external object in two ways imperfectly—namely, *either* explicitly in one, in which the others are objects indeterminately, *or* explicitly in none, but all become objects implicitly while only the most formally signified character is the object explicitly.[8]

8* These statements are not contrary to the teaching of St. Thomas. For *being* is first known in the order of origin by an imperfect concept, but in the order of distinct cognition it is known by a perfect concept.

That *being* has a most simple concept likewise is in agreement with what has been said. For simplicity is opposed to composition, and analogous unity is not unity resulting from composition; therefore, by being analogous, *being* does not have any admixture of composition.

Let us show the resolution [of other concepts into being] by an example. If you wish to resolve *substance* into *being* and want resolution into the distinct concept of being, substance will be resolved into the nature of substance insofar as this nature is the foundation of a 'to be,' which is most simple and to which both substance itself and the transcendentals add [something]. If, however, you wish to resolve [substance] into the confused concept [of being], you will resolve into[9] *what is* and this, too, is most simple and to it, too, susbstance and the transcendentals add [something].

[8]The Zammit edition punctuates as follows: *res significata, extra potest obici dupliciter: imperfecte scilicet vel in uno explicite in quo caetera obiciuntur indeterminate; vel in nullo explicite, sed omnia implicite, in solo formalissimo significato explicite.* The context, however, would seem to require that we punctuate as follows: *dupliciter imperfecte: scilicet vel . . .; vel . . .*

[9]The preposition *in* is lacking in the Latin, but seems required by the context.

9* Fore many there is an occasion of error here because in the distinct resolution they try to resolve into what is analogously *one* in the same way they are used to perform resolutions into what is univocally *one*. Accordingly, just as in univocals, so also in analogy they seek a term, as it were, numerically *one,* although in analogy the term is only proportionably *one*.

Thus each of the resolvable concepts must be resolved into simple objective and mental concepts, and all must be resolved into a simple objective and mental concept which is proportionably *one*. Accordingly, to conclude the discussion in a few words, the statement that *being* is the first concept, into which all resolution is made, and to which all other concepts add something, is to be interpreted by way of analogy. It does not contradict the statement that *being* according to its adequate and perfect concept does not abstract from the predicamental natures, just as no analogon abstracts from the things that gave rise to the analogy.

Conclusion

10* The whole key to clarity in this matter is that one should always remember that everything is said in accordance with what is proper to analogous terms.

I do not think that anything else remains to be said with respect to your question. On the contrary, I have been too verbose for an intellect as keen as yours, which would have understood everything from a single word.

With best wishes, and kindly pray for me.

Rome, February 27, 1509

BIBLIOGRAPHY*

English Works

Anderson, James F., *The Bond of Being. An Essay on Analogy and Existence,* St. Louis—London, 1949.

———, *"Mathematical and Metaphysical Analogy in Saint Thomas,"* in *Theology,* III (1941), pp. 564ff.

Bochenski, I. M., O.P., *"On Analogy,"* in *The Thomist,* 1948, pp. 424ff.

Diggs, B. J., *Love and Being,* New York, 1946.

Esdaille, Byles W., *"The Analogy of Being,"* in *The New Scholasticism,* XVI (1942), pp. 331ff.

Foote, E. T., *"Anatomy of Analogy,"* in *The Modern Schoolman,* XVIII (1940), pp. 12ff.

Joyce, G. C., *"Analogy,"* in *Encyclopedia of Religion and Ethics,* vol. I, New York, 1908, pp. 451ff.

MacIntyre, A., *"Analogy in Metaphysics,"* in *Downside Review,* 1951, pp. 45ff.

Mascall, E. L., *Existence and Analogy,* London, 1949.

Patterson, R. L., *The Conception of God in the Philosophy of Aquinas,* London, 1933.

Phelan, G. B., *Saint Thomas and Analogy,* (The Aquinas Lectures, 1941) Milwaukee, 1943.

Latin Works

Alvarez-Menendez, S., O.P., *"De diversitate et identitate analogica iuxta Cajetanum,"* in *La Ciencia Tomista* (mayo-junio, 1934), pp. 310ff.

Bittremieux, J., *De analogica nostra Dei cognitione et praedicatione,* Louvain, 1913.

Del Prado, N., O.P., *De veritate fundamentali philosophiae christianae,* Fribourg, 1911, pp. 196f. and 499ff.

Descoqs, P., S.J., *Institutiones metaphysicae generalis,* Paris, 1925, vol. I, pp. 206ff.

Joannes a St. Thoma, O.P., *Logica,* II, 13 and 14 (In Reiser ed. of the *Cursus Philosophicus,* vol. I, pp. 478ff.).

*This bibliography is not meant to be complete.

Le Rohellec, J., C. S. Sp., *"De fundamento metaphysico analogiae,"* in *Divus Thomas* (Piacenza), 1926, pp. 79-101 and 664-691.
"Cognitio nostra analogica de Deo," *ibid.*, 1927, pp. 298-319.
Both articles may be found in *Problèmes Philosophiques,* Paris, 1932, pp. 97-162.

Ramirez, J., O.P., *"De analogia secundum doctrinam aristotelico-thomisticam,"* in *Ciencia Tomista,* 1921 (vol. 13) pp. 20-40, 195-214, 337-357; 1922 (vol. 14), pp. 17-38. Published in book form, Madrid, 1922.

Sylvestris Ferrariensis, Fr. de, O.P., *Commentaria in Summa contra Gentiles,* Lib. I c. 34. In Leonine ed. of *Opera Omnia* of St. Thomas.

Suarez, Fr., S.J., *Disputationes metaphysicae,* disp. 2, 28 and 32; in Vivès ed. of *Opera Omnia,* vol. 25, pp. 67ff.; vol. 26, pp. 16ff., pp. 320ff.

To these may be added the usual manuals of scholastic philosophy, such as Gredt, Boyer, Remer, Grenier, etc., etc.

French Works

Balthasar, N., *L'être et les principes métaphysiques,* Louvain, 1914.
"L'abstraction et l'analogie de l'être," in *Estudis Francescans,* 1924, pp. 116ff. or *Revue néo-scolastique,* 1922, pp. 527ff.
L'abstraction métaphysique et l'analogie des êtres dans l'être, Louvain, 1935.

Blanche, F.A., O.P., *"Note sur le sense de quelques locutions concernant l'analogie dans le langage de saint Thomas d'Aquin,"* in *Revue des sciences philosophiques et théologiques,* 1921, pp. 52ff.
"La notion de l'analogie dans la philosophie de saint Thomas," *ibid.*, pp. 169ff.
"Une théorie de l'analogie," in *Revue de philosophie,* 1932, pp. 37ff.
"L'analogie," *ibid.*, 1923, pp. 248ff.

Cazes, M. Fr., O.P., *"La philosophie moderniste,"* in *Revue Thomiste,* 1912, pp. 156ff.

Chollet, A., *Analogie,* in *Dictionnaire de Théologie Catholique,* vol. 1, col. 1142ff.
Anthropomorphisme, ibid., vol. 1, col. 1367ff.

Debraisieux, M., *Analogie et symbolisme,* Paris, 1921.

Desbuts, *"La notion d'analogie d'après saint Thomas d'Aquin,"* in *Annales de philosophie chrétienne,* 1906.

Gardeil, A., *"La structure analogique de l'intellect,"* in *Revue Thomiste,* 1926, pp.

Gentil, P., *"L'analogicité de l'être,* in *Revue Augustin,* July 1909.

Landry, B., *"L'analogie de proportion chez S. Thomas d'Aquin,* in *Revue néo-scolastique,* 1922, pp. 257ff.

"L'analogie de proportionalité chez S. Thomas d'Aquin," ibid., pp. 454ff.

Laurent, E., C.S.Sp., *"Quelques réflexions sur l'analogie,"* in *Acta Pont. Acad. S. Thomae Aq.,* vol. V, 1938, pp. 169ff.

Marc, A., S.J., *"L'idée thomiste de l'être et les analogies d'attribution et de proportionalité,* in *Revue néo-scolastique,* 1933, pp. 157ff.

Moré-Pontgibaud, Ch. de, *"Sur l'analogie des noms divins,"* in *Recherches de science religieuse,* 1929-1930.

Penido, M.T-L., *Le rôle de l'analogie en théologie dogmatique,* Paris, 1931, *Préliminaires philosophiques,* pp. 11ff.

"Cajetan et notre connaissance analogique de Dieu," in *Revue Thomiste,* vol. 17 (1934-1935), pp. 149ff.

Munnynck, M. de, *"L'analogie métaphysique,"* in *Revue néo-scolastique,* 1923, pp. 129ff.

"Intuition et analogie," in *Atti del V Congresso Intern. di Filosofia,* 1925.

Sertillanges, A.D., O.P., *Agnosticisme ou Anthropomorphisme?,* Paris, 1908.

Solages, B. de, *Dialogue sur l'analogie à la Societé toulousaine de philosophie,* Paris, 1946.

Valensin, A., *"Une théorie de l'analogie,"* in *Revue Apologetique,* 1921, pp. 321ff.

Van Leeuwen, A., S.J., *"L'analogie de l'être,"* in *Revue néo-scolastique,* 1936, pp. 293ff. and 469ff.

German Works

Coreth, E., S.J., *"Dialektik und Analogie des Seins,"* in *Scholastik,* 1951, pp. 57-86.

Feckes, K., *Die Analogie in unsern Gotterkennen, ihre metaphysische und religioese Bedeutung,* Muenster, 1928.

Goergen, A., *Kardinal Cajetans Lehre von der Analogie; ihr Verhaeltnis zu Thomas von Aquin,* Speyer, 1938.

M. Grabmann, *"Die Stellung des Cardinal Cajetan in der Geschichte des Thomismus,"* in *Angelicum,* 1934, pp. 547ff. Cf. the revision of the same article in *Mittelalterliches Geistesleben, Muenster,* 1926, vol. II, pp. 602ff.

Habbel, J., *Die Analogie zwischen Gott und Welt nach Thomas von Aquin,* Regensburg, 1928.

M. Limbourg, *"Die Analogie des Seinsbegriffes,"* in *Zeitschrift fuer Katholische Theologie,* vol. IV (1893).

Manser, G. M., O.P., *"Das Wesen des Thomismus,"* in *Divus Thomas* (Fr.) 1928-1931. Contains articles on analogy, in 1928, pp. 385ff.; in 1929, pp. 3ff. and 322ff.; in 1931, pp. 223ff. Also published in book form, Fribourg, 1932.

Przywara, E., S.J., *"Die Reichweite der Analogie als katholischer Grundform,"* in *Scholastik,* 1940, pp. 339ff. and 508ff.

Santeler, J., S.J., *"Die Lehre von der Analogie des Seins,"* in *Zeitschrift fuer katholische Theologie,* 1931, pp. 1ff.

Italian Works

Bellefiore, L., *"Univocità dell'essere e analogia dell'ente,"* in *Revista di Filosofia Neoscolastica,* 1941, pp. 222ff.

"Le basi gnoseo-metafisiche dell'univocità e dell'analogia," ibid., 1942, pp. 191ff.

Petazzi, G. M., *"Univocità od analogia?" ibid.,* 1911-1912, pp. 32ff.

Dutch Works

De analogie van het zijn. Verslag van de VIII° algemeene vergadering der vereniging voor thomistische wijsbegeerte, Nijmegen, 1942.

Dooyeweerd, H., *"De leer der analogie in de thomistische wijsbegeerte en in de wijsbegeerte der wetsidee,"* in *Philosophia Reformata,* 1942, pp. 47ff.

Witte, A. de, O.P., *Analogie,* Roermond-Maaseik, (1946).

Huffer, E.S.J., *"De analoge volmaaktheden in hun verhouding tot het ziin,"* in *Bijdragen uitgegeven door de Philosophische en Theologische Faculteiten der Noord- en Zuid-Nederlandse Jezuieten,* 1947, pp. 268ff.

Walgrave, J. H., O.P., *"Analogie en metaphysiek,"* in *Tijdschrift voor Philosophie,* 1951, pp. 79ff.

Spanish Works

Derisi, O.N., *"Esencia y significado de la analogia metafisica,"* in *La ciencia tomista,* 1949, pp. 298ff.

García López, J., *"La analogia del ser," ibid.,* pp. 607ff.

INDEX OF NAMES AND QUOTATIONS

References are made to the marginal numbers.
Heavy print indicates references or quotations made by Cajetan himself.

---

[1]Books are numbered according to the Ross' translation.
[2]References from one part of *The Analogy of Names* to another are not indicated. Books quoted are arranged in chronological order.

[3]Books quoted are arranged in chronological order.

INDEX OF SUBJECT MATTER*

The references are to the marginal numbers.

*Contains only matter taken from the works of Cajetan. The letter *n* after a number refers to a footnote.

www.ingramcontent.com/pod-product-compliance
Lightning Source LLC
Chambersburg PA
CBHW060420090426
42734CB00011B/2382

* 9 7 8 1 6 0 6 0 8 4 6 3 2 *